Bishop Jackso[n]
Thanks you
many peop[le]
The healer of our wounded Hearts!

Psalm 147:3-5

Jack Redmond

Wounded Heart

Keys to Overcoming Life's Pain and Disappointments

By

JACK REDMOND

Copyright © 2009 by Jack Redmond

Wounded Heart
Keys to Overcoming Life's Pain and Disappointments
by Jack Redmond

Printed in the United States of America

ISBN 978-1-60791-408-2

All rights reserved solely by the author. The author guarantees all contents are original and do not infringe upon the legal rights of any other person or work. No part of this book may be reproduced in any form without the permission of the author. The views expressed in this book are not necessarily those of the publisher.

Unless otherwise indicated, Bible quotations are taken from The Holy Bible New International Version®, Copyright © 1973, 1978, 1984 by International Bible Society, Used by permission of Zondervan, and The King James Version of the Bible, KJV, Copyright © 1994 by The Zondervan Corporation, and The New King James Version, NKJ, Copyright © 1979, 1980, 1982 by Thomas Nelson, Inc., and The Amplified Bible, AMP, Old Testament, Copyright © 1965, 1987 by the Zondervan Corporation, and The Amplified New Testament, Copyright © 1958, 1987 by the Lockman Foundation.

www.xulonpress.com

Dedication

Wounded Heart is dedicated to everyone who has struggled and overcome. I solute those that wake up every day and keep going because of the drive within them. I congratulate all those who decided to not quit and those who have picked themselves up, dusted themselves off and gotten back in the game of life. Life is a journey and the road to victory is traveled one step at a time! Keep steppin!

In this together – Jack

Table of Contents

Chapter 1 - The Reality of Pain 9
Chapter 2 - Trusting God In the Middle of Pain 19
Chapter 3 - Preparing to Move Past the Pain
　　　　　　of Today 27
Chapter 4 - Key 1 – Learn What True Love Is 33
Chapter 5 - Key 2 – Understand How Important
　　　　　　Your Heart Is 39
Chapter 6 - Key 3 – Allow Your Pain & Disappointment
　　　　　　to Drive You to God 45
Chapter 7 - Key 4 – Identify the Cause of Your Pain 51
Chapter 8 - Key 5 – Don't Get Stuck on Stupid 59
Chapter 9 - Key 6 – Learn to Guard Your Heart 67
Chapter 10 - Key 7 – Don't Let the Past Determine
　　　　　　 Your Future 73
Chapter 11 - Key 8 – Let God Direct Your Life 79
Chapter 12 - Key 9 – Let Go! 83
Chapter 13 - Key 10 – Build a Winning Team 87
Chapter 14 - Key 11 – Be a Positive Risk Taker 97
Chapter 15 - Key 12 – Live a Great Life! 103
Chapter 16 - Our Final Goal: Helping Others 107

Chapter 1

The Reality of Pain

Pain is one of the harsh realities of life. It can suddenly smack you in the face or slowly eat away at your soul. Pain is real and we have to deal with it. It comes from the disappointments, failures and conflicts we all have to face. Pain is an equal opportunity affliction that doesn't care about your race, education, experience or position in life. As much as we try to avoid it, pain will eventually pop up on our doorstep. Like an unwanted visitor who won't stop knocking, eventually we have to deal with it.

Over the years I have tried to avoid pain, ignore pain, become immune to pain and even party my way through pain. These were all miserable failures. The reality is that if we ever want to overcome and be free of pain, we must come face to face with its source and begin a healing process towards wholeness and freedom. Life has taught me to acknowledge pain, do what I can to stop the cause and then look it in the face to overcome it. Chances are you have some circumstance or past experience that is still causing you to feel pain or disappointment.

In the pages ahead, we will be taking a journey. On this journey we will look at some keys to overcoming life's pain and disappointments. Pain in life is like the potholes and bumps in the road and is just part of the trip. We can never totally avoid them, but we can make the ride a lot smoother. I know someone who had a choice between two cars. They chose the cheaper one. They told me the car worked fine as long as you didn't mind feeling every single bump in the road! Too many times we try to take the cheap way out and pay for it in the end. To overcome life's pain and disappointment, it will cost you. But as the old commercial says, you can pay me now or pay me later. It will cost to invest in your spiritual growth. It will cost you to become smarter and wiser. It will cost you to make the tough decisions today that may not pay off until the future. Growth always costs.

Wise people don't just waste money, they make investments. Many of us are very careful with our money, but not so careful with other areas of life. Everyday our choices, words and actions are investments. The greater our investment in growing closer to God and bettering ourselves, the less we will feel the painful bumps and potholes in that road called life. Another thing I've learned in life is that many of us are willing to go through hard times if there is a purpose or goal that we are going after. Achieving those goals makes the pain of yesterday and today seem a whole lot smaller and insignificant as we strive towards the meaningful things in life.

God has created us with purpose. That purpose always involves being successful in the things that matter most in life. Success in relationships, on the job, in the family and spiritually are all necessary to live a happy life. *Wounded Heart* is not a book about pain, but about victory. It is not about the pains of yesterday, but the healing and joy that can follow. Healing and wholeness are God's plan for our lives. Wholeness and happiness are a lifestyle. We are only victims if we stay in our place of pain. We are only losers if we accept defeat. We are only hopeless when we try to do everything on our own without the help of God.

The Universal Language – Wasn't It Supposed to Be Love?

They say love is the universal language, but I'm not so sure about that. I've met a lot of people who don't know what love is. When you look around the world there are many people who are filled with hatred or have lived tragic lives and haven't experienced love. But when someone opens up about their pain, an amazing thing happens: people begin to associate with one another because they've been there. Unfortunately, it seems that pain may be the real universal language. Even though pain is a universal experience, there are many who don't know how to overcome pain and move past it. Pain has the ability to paralyze you. It can cause you to live in fear and caution. There was a time in my life when I vowed that no one would ever hurt me. I built a wall around my heart in an effort to protect it. As a result, two things happened. First, I achieved my goal of not letting anyone hurt me. But something worse happened. I armor-plated my heart so much that pain could not get through, but neither could love.

For years, I was incapable of giving and receiving love. I'm so glad that those days are in my past. I'm committed to moving forward and never going back there again! I think there are a lot of people walking around with armor-plated hearts. For many it is a choice, for others it is a matter of survival. God wants us to protect our hearts, but not at the expense of shutting out people who care about us. God's armor consists of things like truth, wisdom, self-respect and making the right decisions.

Allowing Myself to Feel Pain

Eventually, there came a time in my life when I wanted to love and be loved. I had grown so distant from people.

I had relationships, I was successful and I was working on multiple degrees in graduate school at Columbia University. I was living out another one of my dreams and was completely miserable. I felt nothing. I had no emotions left. It began in high school, grew worse in college and now I was at a crossroad in life. I was cold-hearted and didn't let people love me for many years. But I was tired.

I was walking up a steep hill in New York City around Broadway and 123rd Street on a very cold day. The wind was burning my face, and all of a sudden I realized that this was the first time I had felt anything in a long time. I was actually happy to feel the pain–to feel anything. At that moment something hit me and I decided I wanted to live and love again. I accepted the fact that I might have to go through pain. I knew that feeling joy, pleasure and love would only be possible if I were willing to take a chance at being hurt. I was tired of being a tough guy. So the journey began.

They say the longest journey begins with a single step. I took my first step on that cold winter night. I'm still walking and still learning. I have heard people say: "I'm not where I want to be, but I'm not where I used to be!" I'm still on that journey, but it's been a good trip. As I have learned about what true love is over the years, it amazes me how little I really knew about love!

Learning to Live Again

On my journey I cried a lot of tears and searched for many answers. One of the songs I used to listen to was called "Learning to Live Again" (Written by Don Schlitz-Stephanie Davis). A couple of the lines said: "I'm gonna smile my best smile and I'm gonna laugh like it's going out of style. Look into her eyes and pray that they don't see, that learning to live again is killing me." Learning to live again was painful. All the pain I denied now came back. On the outside things looked great to most people. I had everyone fooled but me. Years of pain, disappointment and bad decisions were catching up with me. Another song said: "And I'm cryin' inside, but nobody knows but me." (Written by Kevin Sharp) We have to be careful that we aren't fooled by our outward appearance. We can make our outsides look great, but many times it's just decorations trying to hide how we really feel.

You may be going through a tough time or starting over after a difficult experience. For me, the pain came before the pleasure. The healing came before the wholeness. It's been a difficult journey, but one that I needed to take. I deal with a lot of people who are going through difficult times and the one thing I usually say to them in the beginning is to just keep going. Quitting is too easy and it never works!

Once I was watching MTV and Steven Tyler, the lead singer of Aerosmith, said something profound that I still share with people. He was talking about the ups and downs of life and the interviewer asked him how he made it through the hard times. He said: "The only way out is through." I have seen many people go through horrendous situations and they all have one thing in common. They were determined to make it through.

Choices are powerful things. Many times all it takes in life is a choice and a commitment to following through. Maybe you've been overlooked for that promotion or turned down at job interview after job interview. Stick with your goal and advancement will come. Maybe you've been hurt or abused. God will heal you and give you the wisdom you need to avoid continuing to go through those experiences. Maybe you've wanted a child and you've had multiple miscarriages, but you don't know if you are willing to try again. I know many people who have children who were told they couldn't. My wife was told that she couldn't have children because her uterus is deformed. But today we have four beautiful children. If you're determined, you can go through.

If you don't have the strength, ask God to give it you and He will. God is in the miracle business and the healing business. He's always looking for more people to help!

Cleaning Out the Wounds

When I was growing up, I used to work as a lifeguard at the beach. We had these wooden boardwalks that were famous for the splinters you could get from them. I had the unique talent and responsibility of being the splinter doctor. I could get out any splinter. It was just a matter of skill and perhaps a little bit of digging! People would often ask: "Doesn't it hurt when you do that?" as I dug in to get the splinter. With a smile, I would reply, "No, I don't feel it a bit!" OK, so I struggle with sarcasm. The reality is that in order to get that splinter out, sometimes it was necessary to cause pain to my unfortunate patient. While the digging was going on, it was never a pleasant experience. But inevitably, after the splinter was pulled out, came a sigh and a smile. The pain was necessary for the healing to take place. When splinters stay in they become infected and grow more painful until they are removed.

Everyone once in a while, someone with a splinter would see the tweezers or pin and wouldn't let anyone touch the splinter. Life's broken hearts, failures and disappointments are a lot like those splinters. Sometimes we would rather leave them in than go through the pain involved with removing them. The problem is that life's pain and disappointments can be like those splinters. They will eat away at your soul and cause you to look at life through the pain.

Another example we are all probably familiar with are the skinned knees we got as kids. We'd go home with a bloody knee and mom would pour on the hydrogen peroxide and start to rub the scrape to clean out the dirt. Oh the good old days! Mom knew that we had to clean out that cut so that it could heal. The splinter doctor and mom were great resources, but who do we go to with our wounded heart?

You Better Have a Good Mechanic

When I moved to a new town and got a new car, I needed a mechanic I could trust and who had the right skills. As I looked, I came across a man known as "Scotty G, the Auto MD." I checked him out and he had all the right certifications and experience. His prices were fair and his work was reliable. So life is simple–got a splinter, go to the splinter doctor; skinned knee, go to mom; need a tune up, go to Scotty G the Auto MD!

But where do I go with my wounded heart? I need someone who understands how it works, someone who can fix it and someone I can trust. In my search I found out that there is only one who is qualified and capable of healing my wounded heart. His name is God and He still makes house calls! In the book of Psalms it says this about God: "He heals the brokenhearted and binds up their wounds" (Psalm 147:3).

Some people say that Christians use religion as a crutch, and some do. Jesus is more than religion. He is Almighty God. Jesus is more than a crutch, He is the whole hospital. From the emergency room, to the surgeon, to the rehabilitation, He does it all! Many people are not interested in God because they have seen what so-called religious men have done. I don't want to get too deeply into this right now, but the reality is that many people have misrepresented Jesus. Most of us have been to church services that seemed more like a powerless ceremony than a spiritual connection with and representation of God. Many people who feel like they have rejected God have not. They have rejected a form of religion that has no power. I invite you right now to take a deeper look at Jesus because unlike many of the ceremonies of man, Jesus is the real deal and is able to help you.

Is Time Enough?

They say time heals all wounds, but that has not been my experience. Many wounds take special care. I've had five knee operations, including both knees being "reconstructed" after tearing a major ligament in each. I am so grateful for having a great surgeon and great rehab. During rehabilitation, I switched my college major to Athletic Training, which is a lot like physical therapy but specializes in working strictly with athletes. Today my knees feel great and I am able to do just about anything I want and I expect no knee problems in the days to come.

However, many athletes were not so fortunate in the past. I often meet people who had less serious injuries than I did but because the quality of surgery and rehabilitation were not as good in previous decades, they now have major problems that lead to arthritis and even total knee replacements! Due to a lack of knowledge some people were just left to heal on their own without any follow up rehab.

Too many times we treat our emotional and spiritual wounds with a leave-it-alone-and-it-will-get-better attitude, but like those athletes of old, the injuries stick around and get worse over time. We need to be smarter than that. We need the Great Physician! Since God is the Creator of the heart, He knows how it really works, and His Word says that He can take our broken hearts and heal them. We have several goals in the pages ahead, such as recognizing your hurts and changing your behaviors so that you don't keep getting hurt. But the most important goal is connecting to the Healer. When people come to me after they've been fired, failed at something or been betrayed, I talk with them and comfort them. But most importantly, I point them to Jesus. I understand that I am limited, but God is limitless! When we come to the end of ourselves, we are just getting to the beginning of God. This is something that you must experience for yourself. My goal is to help you connect with God. He will not only heal you, but guide you to make right choices that will help you avoid failures, pitfalls and wrong people. It's about having a relationship with Jesus. He promises that when you seek Him, He will be found! So don't travel this bumpy road alone. Invite God to be part of your journey and surround yourself with people who are for you and not against you.

Yes, pain is a harsh reality, but God is bigger than your pain. With God there is hope. Each day is a new opportunity. The healing of a wounded heart is a journey, so let's get ready to take the next step.

Chapter 2

Trusting God In the Middle of Pain

It is very difficult to trust anyone when we are in pain. Our natural instinct is to protect ourselves. When we trust someone, we must be vulnerable to them. That's what trust is. Trust is letting down your guard to someone who you believe will help and protect you. In times of pain this is hard, if not impossible. I have struggled with trusting people. When people let us down or hurt us at very crucial times in life, it can have a way of burning something into our soul, causing us to not be willing or able to trust others. It is not healthy if we have no one to trust. For me, learning to trust people began with learning to trust God in some painful situations.

It was a Tuesday morning and John was playing his guitar and singing worship songs during a chapel service. I don't remember the song but I remember the pain. It was several weeks after my wife had miscarried twins. We had both dreamed of twins. We had two daughters and everything seemed perfect. We believed these were our twin boys. Our family was complete. Our dreams were coming true.

My wife had been experiencing problems in her pregnancy, including ongoing bleeding, but it never crossed our minds that the twins were not OK because we had been through this before. After another ultrasound, the doctor told her, "Sorry, you lost the babies, there is nothing in your womb anymore." In a moment our dream was gone. *How could this happen, we asked. Is it true? Are you sure?* I felt numb, but I focused on getting my wife through this difficult time. The pain would come later.

When a Dream Dies

I had experienced some major disappointments in my life, but nothing like this. I knew what it was like to work for a goal for years and fall short. I knew what it was to give everything you have to make a relationship work and for it to not be enough, but this was different. I had no control. There was nothing I could do. I wasn't blaming God for it, but why did He let it happen? God is the author of life, not of death. God is love. God is full of grace. He didn't make it happen, but for some reason He let it happen. That's reality.

I had to make a choice. I could be mad at God or trust that He let it happen because something was wrong with the babies or my wife was in danger. God is a God of mercy. But I was in pain and confused, and I was at a crossroad. I love Jesus more than anyone or anything else. He is my source of strength and direction in life. I was trying to work through these facts combined with the reality that my children were gone. I wondered what I should do. I decided to tell God "I trust You!" As I said it, I felt pain shoot through me. It was a pain that I felt in every ounce of my being. It was complete and thorough. I meant what I said. I repeated it, and it was like my insides were being ripped out. I was kneeling and sobbing in pain. I was in a place I didn't understand. Deep down, I still trusted God. It didn't make sense to my mind but in my spirit I knew it was right. Each time I repeated "I trust You," I was consumed by pain.

But something else was happening in my moment of pain. I was entering into a place of freedom. I would not let pain ruin my life. For many people an event like this might lead to marital problems and even divorce. This period of our lives actually brought me and my wife closer together. Trusting God was a painful choice, but it was the best choice.

When You Feel Alone in Your Pain

Even though I had a wife who was going through this terrible time with me and many friends who were there for me, I still felt very alone. I really wasn't able to talk to anyone about it yet except for my God. He was the only one that I could really turn to, even though for some reason He let us lose our babies. I didn't have an answer, I just had reality. I was at a crossroad. I had to make a choice. Would I run to my God or walk away with my pain and unanswered questions? I made a choice to trust God through my pain.

I still don't have an answer, but I do trust God. I've learned to trust Him over the years in both good and bad times. Since this happened, we have had two more children. My wife's dream was always four children. It didn't work out the exact way we would have chosen, but God was faithful. I know that God is a God of love and grace, and these always come first in His actions. I know that somewhere in this situation was an expression of God's love and mercy. I may never have an answer to the "why" question on this side of eternity, so I have chosen to trust Him and continue to move on with life.

I have used the word "chosen" several times for a very important reason. A decision is not necessarily based on emotions. Emotions are very powerful and often consume us. There are times when our emotions can get the better of us and we don't make the choices that are best for us. One thing that I have learned is that if I wait for my emotions to be right or feel good before I act, I very rarely will "feel" my way in to doing the right things that I need to do. I've learned that when I make the right decision, even though it goes against my feelings, eventually my feelings will turn good. In other words, you will seldom feel your way into acting right, but if you complete the right actions, your feelings will eventually catch up and you will benefit from making the right choices. On this painful morning, I chose to trust God.

For almost two months, people continued to come up to me and my wife in church and call to congratulate us on expecting twins. Each time was a painful reminder of our loss. These expressions were from people who love us and care for us but didn't yet know what had happened. The hardest part for my wife was going to church and having to talk to people or listen to what they had to say. For weeks I tried to walk in front of my wife and intercept people before they got to her to congratulate or console her. It was still too soon and the wounds were too fresh, so each comment meant reliving our loss once again. So many times, I would need to ask the Lord for strength and wisdom in dealing with people. I had to share kind words as I explained our loss over and over again, but God was with me. There are many times when scripture only becomes real when you live it. Proverbs says, "Trust in the Lord with all your heart and lean not on your own understanding; in all your ways acknowledge him, and he will make your paths straight" (Proverbs 3:5-6).

Trusting the Lord

Most people read this scripture and picture God as a happy crossing guard who points you in the right direction so that you can continue on your merry way. It can mean this, but it also means that we are to trust God when we don't understand what is going on in life. People often ask themselves questions like: "How did this happen?" or "How did I get into this?" It is in these moments where God becomes more real to us than ever before. He promises to make our paths straight. That is a poetic way of saying that He will lead us in the right and best direction. The issue is that for Him to do that we have to do our part. Our part is to acknowledge Him in all our ways. We often don't receive His direction because we don't really acknowledge Him and seek His input into our lives.

He guides us in many ways, including the Bible. Psalm 119:105 says, "Your word is a lamp to my feet and a light for my path." This basically means that God has given us the Bible to shows us where our next step should be. In today's culture it may mean that His Word is like the headlights in my car that keep me on the road and help me avoid crashing. His Word gives us the rules and principles to live by. Just like those lines on the highway keep us from colliding with other cars, His Word will help us put clear and healthy boundaries in our lives.

Many people are mad at God or feel like He doesn't want to help them in life, when it is actually God's desire to lead us step by step. Too many of us are like the stubborn drivers who don't want to stop and ask for directions when they are lost. Our lives would be much better if we took time out each day to stop and read God's directions in the Bible.

In addition to the Bible, if we have chosen to follow and obey Jesus, God the Father promises us the gift of the Holy Spirit to guide us into all truth (see John 16:13). These are just two ways that God guides us. The more we know the direction He would have us go and the more we follow, the better the journey we will take each day.

With All Your Heart

Many of the promises of God are conditional. He tells us what He will do, but it is up to us to position ourselves to receive what He wants to give us. We would all love for God to constantly direct us in the right way in our decisions and actions. The condition is that we trust Him with all of our heart. The key to total direction is total trust. The funny thing is that we often are so quick to trust our hearts with people who don't take care of them, that by the time we figure out that we need to trust God with our hearts, we are afraid to trust anyone, including God!

We Can't Depend on Our Own Thinking and Wisdom

The second condition is "not leaning on our own understanding." This means that we can not just trust our own thinking, wisdom and decisions. This can be difficult because society teaches us to be self-reliant and that we are weak when we depend on others. The reality is that when we compare ourselves to God, we are weak, lack wisdom and at times are terrible decision makers. We must acknowledge that God knows us and the world around us a whole lot better than we do.

Acknowledging God

God's Word says, "God opposes the proud but gives grace to the humble" (James 4:6). This means that when we acknowledge we need Him, He helps us. When we don't, we are on our own. Even worse, if we are proud, God will even resist our efforts. God's grace means many things. Most commonly, it means His forgiveness, guidance and strength for people, even when they don't deserve it. I thank God that over the years He has helped me so much even at moments when I didn't deserve it. That is how much God loves us.

If we do these things, He promises "to make our paths straight." He will show us the right way to go. We need to begin walking on this road even in the middle of our pain. I have had to follow God in some of the worst moments. Sometimes we have to make a decision to not be paralyzed by our pain. Even if you're not ready to limp forward yet, get ready to be ready! Sometimes we need to crawl before we can walk.

Chapter 3

Preparing to Move Past the Pain of Today

For many of us, pain has become a constant companion. It has become part of our lives and just seems normal. This is not God's will or plan. He is not the source of our pain, but He is the one who helps us overcome it and be healed from it. The more intentional we are in overcoming and moving past our pain, the sooner and deeper our healing will be. The first step is in not accepting the pain. Your pain may be fresh or years old, but it has to go. Let's get ready for that journey. It may take time and will probably be painful along the way, but it is a road we have to travel.

Disappointment, failure, rejection, betrayal and broken dreams can wound your heart. This can be temporary or go on forever! Notice I said "temporary." I know what a wounded heart feels like. I know that the pain does not go away by itself, and I know that there is Someone who can heal that wounded heart. You may not know God as a healer but He is. We have a loving God who cares about you and wants to heal your heart if it's been wounded. We often try to heal our wounded hearts ourselves through many different things. If you're anything like me, you've tried to heal your own heart and found out you couldn't. But there is Someone who can! If you're dealing with pain in your heart, be encouraged. Tomorrow can be different and better than today.

You Need a Specialist

In life we often go to specialists when we have a problem. If our car is acting funny, we go to a certified mechanic. When we break a bone we go to a doctor called an orthopedist, because he is a certified bone doctor. So who do we go to when our heart is broken? I don't mean to be offensive, but Oprah can't heal your broken heart! God is THE Specialist when it comes to healing. He is THE Healer. You may be skeptical now, but go ahead and ask Him to heal your heart as you read this book. I am confident that as you understand God more and ask Him to heal you, He will! You have nothing to lose and a whole lot to gain, so go for it. You'll be glad you did.

Why Do Our Hearts Get Wounded?

Everybody's heart is made out of mush. No, I'm not talking about that stuff that babies eat before they can eat real food. I'm talking about our hearts. No, not the one that pumps blood and all that other stuff; I'm talking about our feelings, our emotions, who we really are when you take all of the other stuff away.

You know that "I'm in love" heart; that "I love the beach and the warm sunny breeze" heart. You know that feeling inside when you see a friend or family member you haven't seen for a long time. You know the heart that hurts when you get disappointed after someone lets you down, or when someone isn't there for you when they're supposed to be. You know the heart that is so easily hurt but still wants to feel love again and again. That heart! You know the one

I'm talking about, and when you get through all the exterior toughness and independence, there it is underneath, a big pile of mush! It's amazing how wise and strong people think they are. "I can handle it. I know what I am doing," and many other comments like these are thrown around all the time. Unfortunately, as the Bible says, "pride goes before destruction, a haughty spirit before a fall" (Proverbs 16:18).

But I'm tough, you may be thinking. Yeah, you and me both. I thought I was the toughest thing to ever walk the face of the planet. Don't you hate when you find out you're wrong? It's funny that it doesn't matter what the outside looks like, the heart is still very fragile. You can be physically strong, you can be tough, you may look like nothing will ever bother you or could ever hurt you, but you know as well as I do that the thing we call our heart is really delicate. Hey, don't worry. You can be honest. I won't tell anyone. So why are our hearts so soft?

Your heart is soft, delicate and fragile. But it is also wonderful and capable of feeling so many awesome things. Imagine your heart is like a sponge. The reason a sponge can work is because it is soft. Because it is soft, it can absorb things. Also, because a sponge is soft, you can squeeze it and out comes whatever was absorbed. Just like a heart! A heart must be soft so that it can absorb love. It also must be soft so that it can be squeezed, like from a big hug, and the love can be given away.

Have you ever tried to wipe something up with a completely dry sponge? It doesn't work very well and can't absorb or be squeezed out. It only works when it is a little moist. Too many times, our hearts are hurt and become dried up and cannot absorb or give away love. When we learn how to take care of our hearts, we can keep them from drying up and causing us to live with no joy, hope, happiness or hunger to live life to the fullest. My hope is that we can learn how to live our lives in such a way that our hearts do what they are supposed to do.

What's a Heart for Anyway?

So what are our hearts supposed to do? Hearts are supposed to give and receive that wonderful thing we call love. We can feel this love in our families, with our friends and in that most exciting way in romance. Notice that I listed friends and family first. These are the places where we should learn about what love really is. If we don't learn what true love is from our family and friends, when it comes time for that romantic type of love, man will we be confused. Unfortunately, many times this confusion can result in accepting a counterfeit type of love because we don't really understand what true love is. Ouch! That's a recipe for a broken heart. Our hearts are also a place where we hold all of our dreams and goals for our lives. In a nutshell, our hearts are where we keep the things that matter most to us.

Beautiful, Fragile, Priceless

I have one more example of what a heart is like. Your heart is like a beautiful crystal, finely cut, thin vase. Even if you're a 6-foot, 3-inch middle linebacker, that describes your heart! Back to the vase: It is finely crafted, has great detail and is very valuable. Now if I took that vase and slammed it on the ground, what would happen? It would break into a million pieces. So we should just make sturdier vases, right?

Imagine this. My wife's favorite flowers are tulips. When I buy my wife flowers, I will usually get her a dozen tulips. Just imagine if I was afraid of putting them inside a beautiful, fragile vase because I was afraid it would break. What if instead, on my way home, I pulled over to the side of the road and picked up a dirty, ugly rock, chipped a hole in it for the flowers, threw it in the back of my pickup truck and brought it home. On the way, I think about my new boulder vase with great pride. It will never break, we can have it forever and my wife will love it! Imagine that I walk into the house with those beautiful flowers in that dirty, old, ugly rock that I decided to turn into a vase. I've never tried it, but I don't think that my wife would appreciate my creativity and everlasting vase.

So what do I really do? I put those flowers in that fragile and beautiful vase. Why? Because it is beautiful! The thing that makes that vase beautiful is that it is fragile, it is delicate and it needs to be taken care of—otherwise it will be broken. Our hearts have been made in the same way. The thing that makes our hearts beautiful is that they are fragile, they are special, they are delicate, they are easily broken and they are very valuable. And I say to you that the reason that you can be a beautiful person is because you have been made with a beautiful heart. Your heart is beautiful, it is priceless and it is fragile—and so are you!

Let's continue our journey and look at some keys to experiencing healing in your wounded heart and learning how to protect it in the days to come.

Chapter 4

Key 1 – Learn What True Love Is

Our world is full of "experts." We can turn on the radio, TV or go to the bookstore to hear or read great advice from the "experts." It is amazing how many of yesterday's experts are now seen as flawed or even flat out wrong. The world is full of marriage experts who are on their second or third marriage! I couldn't believe it when I heard that the son one of the greatest "child experts" committed suicide. I think that we are often too quick to accept things we hear as good advice from whoever is most popular. So the question is, "Who do we go to when we want to understand the heart?"

Science teaches us that everything that is organized and has a specific design and purpose needs a creator—someone who planned it and put it together. That creation is designed to work a certain way, under certain conditions, and be maintained a certain way. (And you thought this book was going to be all about that gooey, holding hands, walking-on-the-beach-at-sunset kind of stuff. We'll get to that later, but we won't ever be able to enjoy that if we don't first understand what love really is and how it works in our lives. Enough with the science, let's get back to your heart.)

Since our heart works in a certain way, someone made it that way. The one who made it is God, the Creator of heaven and earth and the entire universe. That same God created you with emotions, feelings, needs and the ability to experience great joy. Something else is true: The heart not only has the ability to experience great joy, but it can also experience great pain. You can't have one unless you have the possibility of the other. God made your heart to work in a certain way, and though we can't understand everything about it, we can learn some basics that will help us to live an awesome life.

We must understand that God created love. He created us so that we are capable of knowing Him in a personal way and experiencing His love. Not only did He create love, but the Bible teaches us that He *is* love. That means His character, or who He is, is love. You can't separate Him and love, it is His essence.

This might sound weird, but if you think about that, it makes sense. Here's what I mean. What is a chocolate bar? It is a bar made of chocolate. When you eat it, what do you eat? You eat chocolate! When you know God in a personal way, what do you know? You know love, and I mean true love. You don't just experience something, you get to know the real thing. Once you know what really good chocolate is there's no substitute. If I took a piece of dark brown plastic and told you it was chocolate and that you should eat it, what would you do? You would probably look at me like I was crazy and not eat it! Likewise, once you really know what true love is, you will never settle for the fake love that many people will offer you! Even if your heart has been wounded by something other than a lack of love, you will still need God's love to heal whatever disappointment or setback that you have experienced.

Getting Ahold of True Love

True love is learned from God. I'm not talking about religion, going to church or sitting in a Sunday school class. All of these things can help us, but they can never substitute for actually knowing and understanding God's love. It goes back to this, if we don't know and understand true love, we will be empty and accept the closest thing that seems like true love. The only problem is that fake love is like eating that brown piece of plastic instead of that yummy chocolate! Counterfeits always look good until you realize that they are not the real thing, and then bang—a wounded heart. I've had both broken bones and broken hearts and let me tell you something, broken bones heal faster!

One of the things that we will talk about later is how to avoid getting our heart broken. I'm not saying that I can give you some formula so that you will never be disappointed or get your heart broken. Actually, I don't think that I would want that guarantee. I feel this way for two reasons. The first reason is that I tried to make my heart break proof. That was a disaster! And second, to live life to the fullest means we have to take chances. When we take chances, we open ourselves up to disappointments and wounded hearts. I would never want to be afraid to take risks. That would mean a boring and nonproductive life. However, I think living life to the fullest does mean not taking foolish chances or trusting our hearts to people or situations that we can be pretty sure will end in a bad way.

When the most important thing in our life is our personal relationship with Jesus, this allows us to walk in confidence and peace. Jesus wants to meet our deepest relational needs. When this takes place in our lives, we are not in a hurry to attempt to fill these needs with people who may let us down. We are free to take our time and proceed at our own pace. We can be more selective, wiser and more willing to walk away from people who don't have our best interest at heart. So how do I guard against future wounded hearts? The answer to that is simple: Learn what true love is and don't accept anything less. Now most people don't know what true love is, and there aren't a whole lot of people teaching us what it is. But we need to know what true love is so that we can know what we are looking for.

So What Does True Love Look Like?

True love does two things: It protects and provides. There are many different things that we call love, but love is much more than a feeling or sensation. In its purest and most powerful form, love is a choice and it is action. What we do is much more powerful than what we feel. Feelings come and go. True love doesn't change like the wind. If you want to know if someone loves you, just watch what they do. Do they protect you from things that would harm you and provide you with the things that you need like friendship, companionship, support and encouragement? Just think about that a little and remember that true love does two things: It protects and it provides. Here is an example.

I have a baby girl. She will often scream and cry in the middle of the night. Do I love her? Absolutely! How do I know? I know because of what I will do. I will lose sleep, clean up stuff I don't want to clean up and give her affection when everything in me doesn't want to. You see, true love is about action not feeling. When it is 4 a.m. and the third time I've gotten up during the night, let me tell you that I am not overwhelmed by warm and fuzzy feelings towards my little darling! But I am driven to meet her needs.

One more story, when my wife was pregnant with our second child, I was in seminary in addition to a very heavy workload. For a season I was getting up at 4:30 each morning to go to work early so that I could get home to help her as soon as I could.

There were times when it was 9 p.m. and there was a sink full of dishes (and our dishwasher had broken). At that point I had been going nonstop for about 17 hours and the only thing I wanted to do was go to sleep. But then I'd see the dishes. One of my wife's greatest pet peeves is dirty dishes in the sink in the morning. So why would I do the dishes when what I really wanted to do was go to bed? Because of love. It is a choice. My feelings would say leave the dishes, but love caused me to dig a little deeper and do something that would help my wife. I would get nothing out of it for myself except knowing that her life was made a little easier the next day. True love is a choice and an action.

This is the type of love that God has for us. He didn't just give us a philosophy or advice on how to live, He sent His only Son to literally die in our places so that we could know Him for ourselves. Jesus went to the cross knowing the pain He would suffer, but was driven by a love so powerful that He chose the pain and suffering to release and demonstrate true and pure love to people like you and me who desperately need it. It is through God's love that we begin to value ourselves and our hearts as much as God does.

Chapter 5

Key 2 – Understand How Important Your Heart Is

With a house full of small children, we have to constantly make sure that we are not leaving valuable items around. We had a brand new cell phone disappear. Brand new bottles of lotion, hair care products and soap will get dumped out or smeared on the wall. We have had walls, doors and television sets written on with pen, markers and crayons. Jewelry, remote controls, computers and electronic games have been lost, damaged and even broken. Little children have no concept of how valuable things are. Just like these wonderful, precious children, we often don't have a proper understanding of how important our hearts are and how we should protect and care for them.

God cares very much about your heart. It amazes me that God cares about my heart more than I care about it myself. This may sound strange but it is very true for many people. If you look around the world you see many people giving their hearts away to just about anybody. So many individuals are walking around with low self-esteem, while others may be quite proud of themselves but don't have any regard for how they live and the consequences down the road. Many of us need to learn to value our hearts. Like a small child who doesn't know the difference between cheap plastic jewelry and the real thing, we often don't value our heart for it's true worth.

God cares about us so much that He came to earth and lived in the flesh to demonstrate His love for us and what it means to live in love day in and day out. In addition to Jesus walking the dirt roads of Israel, God inspired men to write the Bible, which tells the story of God's love and plan from creation into eternity. In the Bible God made sure to focus on teaching us about our hearts and how important they really are.

The Bible is not just any book. It is the most powerful book ever written. It is the best selling book of all time! Every year, more copies of the Bible are printed and sold than any other book. That's not a bad track record. The Bible is God's gift to us. It teaches us about how the world was created; how we can personally know God; and how we can live a life of peace, joy and prosperity. No wonder so many people read it!

I have a program on my computer that lets you put in a word and it tells you every scripture in the Bible with that word in it. There are different translations of the Bible since the original Bible wasn't written in English. For this study I looked in the New International Version, or NIV for short. It lists the word "heart" 570 times, the word "hearts" 209 times and even "broken heart" twice. That's 781 times that God talks to us about our heart. That lets me know that God is concerned about my heart, and your heart, too. Since He made us and our hearts, I think it's important for us to hear what He has to say!

Another way I know He is concerned is because God has healed my wounded heart. I have had many disappointments in my life and each one hurt. Sometimes the pain can be small and it doesn't really bother us. Other times, it can absolutely feel like our heart is being torn in half. I've been through broken relationships and have been disappointed by friends and family. I've worked really hard to achieve something and failed, or just not been good enough. All those things hurt.

Sometimes it doesn't even matter how many things go right, it's the things that go wrong and hurt our hearts that can stick with us. Through all those disappointments, I had an empty feeling inside that I couldn't fill. The more I tried to fill it, the more I couldn't. Talk about frustrating. Even good things couldn't fill it! So I guess like a lot of people, I kept looking for answers. Each time I looked in the wrong place–wham! Another wounded heart. Here I go again!

I tried to succeed my way to happiness through work, education, relationships and great experiences. It amazes me that no matter where disappointment comes from, it's our heart that gets hurt. One of the most painful realities of life is that you can achieve a great goal, succeed in an important area of life or experience the thrill that you thought would fulfill you, but it still doesn't make you happy.

Then the day came in my life when someone told me about how much God loved me and that I was created to have a relationship with Him. Man did that seem weird. If God loved me so much, I thought, then why did I have to go through all this junk? I later came to understand that most of that junk was my choice. Someone told me that God loved me so much that He sent His Son Jesus, down to earth to die on a cross to pay for my sins so that I could personally know and understand how much God loved me. It was my sin that was causing me to make bad choices, which were the cause of most of my pain. Even though I only have one heart, I found out it could be hurt a whole lot of times. I learned that my own choices made God seem far away, but He wanted me to come to Him and would help and care for me with a never ending love. The other reality I learned was that without God's love, the greatest achievement or pleasure quickly slipped away or didn't mean anything to me at all.

The Love I Had Been Looking For

I had been looking for someone to love me in a way that I could never lose. This is the way that God loves us. I was also tired of always trying to be important, smart, successful, funny, or just good at everything. I found out that God loved me not for what I did, but just because of who I am. What a relief! I don't have to impress God. He just loves me unconditionally. I never found that kind of love anywhere else. When I was asked if I wanted to have a personal relationship with Jesus, I said, "Yeah, if it's everything you say it is!" So I prayed that God would forgive my sins, be Lord of my life, and help me to live for Him and to know and understand His love.

I didn't understand everything right away, but things started to change. I began to read the Bible a lot and it seemed like whatever my struggle or question was, God had an answer or way to overcome the struggle. I began to pray and worship God through singing songs. Something began to happen as I felt God's love and presence in my life. Over time I began to live in peace. God fulfilled my need for love and I stopped looking for people to love me in ways that only God could. Over time, God took the pieces of my wounded heart and put them back together. Not only that, but since He taught me what true love is, I began to recognize what is *not* true love. This helped me make better choices for selecting friends and eventually prepared me to fall in love with my wife and get married.

I just want to end this chapter by saying this: God cares about your heart. God Himself taught me what love really is. Not only that, but He also healed my wounded heart in ways that I never could. He showed me how to look for and recognize the type of people who would love me as a friend and as a husband. God does not have favorites. He loves each and every one of us. Whatever He did for me, He has done with many people before me and He can do it for you, too!

I came to Jesus not caring about myself or my heart. God continues to teach me about love and that my heart is very important. Proverbs 4:23 says, "Above all else, guard your heart, for it is the wellspring of life." That means the life you live will come from your heart. If you want to live a good life, you must learn how important your heart really is. From there, you will learn how to guard it as something precious. In addition to guarding it, you may also be in need of healing to take place. Let's see how that happens.

Chapter 6

Key 3 – Allow Your Pain & Disappointment to Drive You to God

On our journey to healing, we have two choices. We can allow our pain and disappointment to either drive us to God or drive us away from God. We can either begin to know God as the Healer or have growing feelings of bitterness or distance from God. It really is a choice. God is available but we have to choose to go to Him. I have seen people take both roads. I have taken both roads. In my own experience, the one that leads to God is the better road. It is not always an easy road, but it is always a better road.

I don't know of anything that can heal wounded hearts besides God. Time may make the pain seem less and we always have to move on in life. We can achieve things that may make up for past failures and that can help. We can begin new relationships, but many times there are things from the past that just "pop up" from time to time, that can reignite all kinds of negative memories and feelings.

I got to a point where I just wanted to start over again. One of the things that was frustrating in my life was that I felt like I had started over so many times. Each time I started over, it was just a matter of time until I was starting over again. I felt like one of those little hamsters running like crazy on his wheel but getting nowhere! It also seemed like past disappointments kept piling up and that was just what life was going to always be like. So in some ways, I was tired of starting over because I had done that so many times. I wanted to really start over again. I wanted to wipe away the past and start brand new without all of the old mess and past hurts of life.

But how in the world is that possible? I found out that it was. It wasn't easy, but it was worth it. I took all of my past hurts and laid them at the cross of Jesus Christ and asked God to help me with them. You see, Jesus didn't die on the cross just to pay for my sins, but also so that I could be healed—physically, spiritually and emotionally. God teaches us about His promises and His character in the Bible. When we read it, believe it through faith and ask God to do it, He will! Let's look at just three verses of Scripture. If you believe them, your whole life can be changed. Here they are: "He heals the brokenhearted and binds up their wounds. He determines the number of the stars and calls them each by name. Great is our Lord and mighty in power; His understanding has no limit" (Psalm 147:3-5).

Tape Up That Broken Heart

I used to work as an athletic trainer in college, high school and for a short time during an NFL summer camp. The athletic trainer is the guy who runs on the field when someone is hurt and checks out the injured player to make a decision on what to do. First, you evaluate the seriousness of the injury. You have to figure out if you can handle it or if you need a doctor. At football games, there was always a doctor that would check the player out if I felt the person had a significant injury. The next choice is to let the athlete get up or make them stay down. If they could get up, then you would take them to the sideline for further evaluation and decide whether or not they could play again or if they needed to get an x-ray or something else.

Other times, I had to make a decision not to move the athlete because of the injury. Many times, I would apply a splint to the injured athlete before moving him. The reason I did that was to stabilize the injury for two reasons. First, if you move an injured athlete before stabilizing the injury, you could make the injury worse. Second, stabilizing the injury helps start the healing process. Another word for stabilizing the injury is binding the injury.

Healing Takes Time

Remember Psalm 147:3 — "He heals the brokenhearted and binds up their wounds." You see, wounded hearts take time to heal. In the meantime, God promises not only that He will heal them, but that He will bind up their wounds. That means He will wrap them up to stabilize them and allow them to start the healing process. It doesn't say that He will say some magic words and poof, all better. It says that He will wrap them up along with other wounds. How does He do that? He wraps them in His love and presence. When an athlete has his leg in a splint, it reminds him that he is not ready to play sports again until it is healed.

Just a piece of advice: When your heart is wounded, it needs to be wrapped up and splinted in God's love for a sufficient amount of time. If you take it out of that protection and throw it back into another romance or another potentially harmful situation, it's just like an athlete with a sprained ligament or broken bone returning to the field too soon. The result is usually reinjuring that body part, and many times injuring it much worse or possibly damaging it for life. In the same way that we need to use wisdom with physical injuries, we need to use wisdom with injuries to the heart.

The same is true if we have failed at something. We should never quit trying in life, but it is often wise to take time to evaluate why we failed so that we can move forward with new wisdom learned through the pain of our experience.

After your heart has been broken, give it enough time to heal before giving it to someone or something else. How long is that? It depends on who you are, what happened and the chance you are willing to take. Just like an athlete going through rehabilitation, you should start slow and build your way up until you are ready to go full speed once again. This means making sure you can trust people. This applies to all people—best friends, classmates and even family. Notice, I didn't go into the boyfriend/girlfriend thing. The winning formula for successful relationships is putting God first, then family, then friends and then romance. If our relationships with God, family and friends are strong we won't be as needy when it comes to romance. If we are emotionally needy, we will expect too much and not be relaxed so that we can build a healthy relationship. After the healing process has taken place, we will hopefully be returning stronger than ever before and this time with a little more wisdom!

Can God Really Do All That for Me?

Yes! God can do all that and a whole lot more! You have to remember who we are dealing with. We are dealing with the Almighty God! Psalm 147:4 says, "He determines the number of the stars and calls them each by name." Scientific law teaches us that matter can't be created or destroyed. That means that the creation of everything was a miracle! If God is powerful enough to create all of the stars in all of the universes, can he help one person with a wounded heart? He sure can. I have seen God heal pains in my life that I thought

I could never overcome. I'm not talking theory, I'm talking about my life. I have learned that I can trust God and what His Word says, and so can you!

But You Don't Understand How I Feel!

Have you ever said that? Let me be honest with you. There is no way someone can fully understand how you feel, but there is someone who does. There are times when I don't understand how I feel! But look at Psalm 147: 5, which says "Great is our Lord and mighty in power; his understanding has no limit. God is mighty in power." This is the God who heals the broken-hearted and binds up our wounds. How strong is He? He is mighty in power! He is strong enough to heal a wounded heart! Does He understand? His Word declares that His understanding has **no** limit. That means He understands!

So many times we expect people to help us who are limited in power and understanding. No wonder we often feel like no one understands or can help us. But God Himself wants to help us. The Word does not promise that He might help us; it talks about what He does. He helps us and He understands all things. In fact, He is the only one who can really understand. Other people may truly care, but we know the truth. They don't really understand. But God does and I'm glad that He is on my side!

God's Promise and God's Character

He heals the broken-hearted! I don't know about you, but I tried to heal my broken hearts with new relationships, new activities, new experiences, greater education, new jobs and many other ways. I even tried to numb the pain with partying. None of it worked! Only when I came to God did healing take place. God's character is that He is a healer.

His Word teaches us that He heals broken hearts. So if you have a broken heart, take it to the one who made it. He is the expert, He knows everything about it and He knows how to heal it!

Chapter 7

Key 4 – Identify the Cause of Your Pain

I ended the last chapter by saying that God could heal "your" broken heart. That may seem like I am assuming that your heart has been wounded. It amazes me at times the amount of pain that people like you and me carry around with us each day. Just about everyone has been through a significant painful season of life. Our hearts can be hurt by a lot of different things. Many times we think about broken hearts from a romantic point of view. This is only one way that our hearts can be wounded. If we are going to have healthy emotions and a healthy outlook on life, we have to live life with our heart and soul in a place of peace. This means identifying events and situations that have hurt us in the past or that we are currently going through. I have worked with people who lived in abusive situations. Their goal was to be free and healed of past pain but they couldn't do that because of their living situation. Their first step to healing and wholeness was moving out! This may seem difficult, but at times is absolutely necessary. I have seen others stay in an abusive situation and watched it destroy them over time.

Other patterns may have to be broken. Some people expect to fail because of past experiences or what they have been told throughout life, especially while growing up. We are shaped by the voices that we listen to. Many people grow up hearing negative things and they allow their lives to be shaped and defined by this negativity. We have to begin to study God's Word and allow Him to define us, not someone else who was speaking through their own pain.

I work with teens and over the years have seen many disappointments and broken hearts. In my opinion, the two things that break teens' hearts the most are parents and best friends. So many times parents let their children down. I'm not trying to parent bash because most parents are doing the best they know how, but some still may let their kids down. This is part of life. Other times, parents just let their kids down because they're not around enough, break promises or they don't meet their child's need for love and affection. Another big issue is that children feel like they are rated on a performance basis for love. They feel like their parents only love them if they do certain things. The problem with this type of love is that it is conditional, and they feel like if they don't meet the standard, then they don't get the love.

Parents Can Be Real Heart Breakers

Let me start off by saying that parents are the most important people in the lives of children and teens! They have the most important job in the world and possibly the hardest. Most parents I know are very good people who work really hard and do their best. Many are doing a great job. Unfortunately, there are others who do not do a good job or are absent from their children's lives. In our society there are also many other situations such as divorce, single parent households and blended families. I would also like to say that some of the best parents I have seen are single parents. Keep up the good work!

Since parent's jobs are so important and they are so close to their teens, they also have the ability to wound hearts very easily. The reason we need to address this is because if we don't, people don't get healed and can walk around with bitterness for years and even decades. I know of people who are 50 and 60 years old who are carrying around the scars and pain of things that happened in their teen years! I have also seen God do amazing things in people's lives. Sometimes this results in a greater family relationship. Other times it just means that an individual is healed of past pain. I have worked with youth who were angry at a father they never met. I have been asked, "How can I forgive someone I have never met?" I have also been asked, "How can I forgive someone who has hurt me, is not sorry and has not changed?" These are difficult questions but are very important ones. The first thing I would say is that forgiveness is not about the other person, it is about you. Holding onto unforgiveness is bad for you. Bitterness and anger have a way of eating away at you mentally, spiritually and even physically. We need to forgive others for ourselves. Forgiveness sets you free to live your life.

Forgiveness also is different and separate from reconciliation. Reconciliation means that you enter back into a healthy and life giving relationship with the person who has hurt you. That is not possible sometimes when the person refuses to change and continues to do things that will hurt us or is absent or deceased. There are things that are outside of your control, and you can drive yourself crazy trying to change things that you don't have power to change.

People rarely change because we want them to. Many times the only way people change is when God does the changing. All we can do is ask God to heal us and change us to be able to withstand certain situations and pray for those who may have hurt us or are still hurting us. Jesus told us to pray for our enemies and those who persecute us. He even told us to love our enemies. I have found in my life that when I pray for people who hurt me or even people I don't like, God changes me first. After I have been changed, I look at the situation differently. The situation didn't change, but my ability to go through it changed dramatically.

Summer Camp Group Discussion

Having worked with teens and families for over a decade, I have heard and seen a lot of things. It can be very hard to get teens to talk and open up in group settings. One-on-one conversations are a lot easier to do. Each year we go on a three-day summer camp. The two main goals of this camp are for the kids to grow closer to God and closer to each other. A couple of summers ago, we got into a discussion about parents. Let me tell you something, teens sure are experts in knowing what parents do wrong! We had just finished speaking about the importance of honoring our parents. That's always a big hit with teens.

Then we began a discussion about this and while some complaints were not legitimate, others were. The thing that struck me was the amount of pain that some teens felt because of their parents. During our discussions, teens can ask or say whatever they want. In response to one comment, one of my leaders was stressing the importance of honoring parents in all situations and you could feel the tension in the air. I agreed with his comments but I added something. I said, "I can see that a lot of you have been caused pain by your parents and I want to let you know that I know that your pain is very real." When I acknowledged the reality of their pain, something broke and a tremendous time of discussion and prayer followed. I learned that one of the biggest causes of wounded hearts is parents. I have also seen that if people do not forgive their parents, they can literally carry anger and unforgiveness with them the rest of their lives.

Many problems in marriages are caused by unresolved wounded hearts and disappointments from things that occurred during childhood and teenage years. An individual then judges events or their spouse based on past experiences. This is why even when you're a teen, you need to come to God, receive healing of your heart and learn to forgive parents who have hurt you. If you're an adult who is still carrying pain, you must let it go if you want to live life to the fullest. Remember, there are times when forgiveness is just for you. You can't change the past, but you can change the future. Bring that pain to God. Let Him take it and heal you. If you don't, you will carry it with you. I know people who were divorced 20 or 30 years ago and still carry the bitterness with them. This pain affects all of the other relationships in their lives. I don't want to belittle pain, but I do want to see people free to live and love once again.

No One Understands Me!

"But you don't understand how I feel!" You're right, I don't understand, but we have a God that does. Some people would say, "Why would a God who loves me allow these things to happen?" It is never God's will for people to treat you poorly. He gives people free will, and sometimes they misuse that and treat others badly, disappoint them or even abuse them. God has given us rules to love one another and for parents to take care of their children in the right way. Pain is not caused by God, but by people's actions and choices.

Best Friends Can Be Real Heartbreakers

When people fight with or lose their best friends, it can be devastating emotionally. Sometimes this is caused by one person just being mean to another. Best friends can be some of our closest relationships, and therefore these friends can have access to areas of our heart that others don't. Sometimes emotional wounds occur when a person makes a mistake and their friend doesn't forgive them afterwards. Either way, we need to know that these things cause wounded hearts and we must overcome them to move on in life and be healthy mentally and emotionally.

Failure Can Be a Real Heartbreaker

Another source of broken hearts is not achieving a specific goal. One of the greatest disappointments in my life was when I didn't win a state championship in football my senior year in high school. This was devastating to me. I had never worked so hard in my life for anything. I had never been so focused. I had never wanted anything more. It seemed at the time like it was more important than life to me. We lost our first two games and won the next seven. We were a very good team but missed the state playoffs by a small margin in the ratings. It was the worst thing that ever happened in my life and I really felt like there was no point to life anymore. Seems a bit dramatic, doesn't it? But hey, I was 17. It may seem silly to you but it was very real to me. It took years for me to get over it. That's right, years. You may have a similar story or possibly one that is very different, but you can associate with my pain.

This disappointment began a lifestyle of anger and a constant need to win or be superior. Getting my way or being better than others became a way of life because I hated failure. I eventually turned into a selfish person who always had to get his way. The next stage was that I pretty much got all the things I wanted and succeeded in achieving just about all of my goals. The problem was that none of those achievements satisfied me. I started down the wrong road because of the pain of failure and disappointment and I just kept going for years even when everything was going my way.

If we ever want to be healed of our wounded hearts, we may have to stop, call a time-out in life and deal with the things that hurt us. You see, before I wanted that championship, I wrestled with feeling like I was never good enough. It wasn't about football at all. I had to stop going down this path and ask God to teach me how valuable I truly was. Fast forward four years. The day came when I won a conference championship in college football. Near the end of the game I was covering a punt and as I was trying to tackle the receiver, I tried to change direction at full speed and felt a pop in my knee. I stood on the sideline in tears knowing that my football career was over because this was my second major knee injury. The championship that I had wanted more than anything was meaningless because I knew that I would never play football again. My addiction to success and approval had grown and changed. It is amazing how much time and energy we expend chasing after things that really have no eternal or even long-lasting benefits in our lives.

So we can see that many different things can cause a wounded heart—anything that causes disappointment, broken trust, neglect or even abuse. It doesn't matter so much where the wounded heart comes from, just that it's there and we have to deal with it. The first step in dealing with it, is getting "unstuck" or off that road that is going in the wrong direction.

Chapter 8

Key 5 – Don't Get Stuck on Stupid

(stop repeating the same mistakes or walking on the same painful path!)

I'm not trying to insult anyone, but let's get real for a minute. How many people do you know who have made the same stupid mistakes and decisions over and over again? How many people are stuck in a difficult situation and don't have the strength or knowledge to get out of it? Others just keep walking down the same painful path not knowing that God can heal the pain or even put them on a new road in life. You may even be in a place where you personally didn't do anything wrong. Somebody else hurt you in some way. You may have to get unstuck from the pain caused by someone else's careless, stupid or mean act.

In your life, how many things would you go back and do differently? If you are like me the answer is plenty. Today, you are probably a lot smarter than you used to be and have probably stopped some bad habits or stopped repeating things that you used to do that were not good for you. You have already gotten off the "stupid treadmill" in some areas of your life. It may be time to get off the "stupid" and get on the "wisdom and smart" path in some other areas. What's strange in life is that we can have 95% of our lives in order and just 5% stuck on stupid. The unfortunate reality is that depending on what areas of life we struggle with, the 5% can ruin the 95% that is going good. Let's face the 5% of stuck on stupid so we can really enjoy the 95% that is going good.

It is amazing how many people do things that they know are wrong or will hurt them. Others are making lifetime decisions without really thinking about the long-term benefits or consequences of their choices. Many decisions are made based on what looks or feels good instead of on what will actually have good results in the end. We live in a society that is emotion driven. It is dangerous when we live by how we feel instead of living our lives based on established principles and wisdom.

Many people don't have principles that they are committed to. Instead they have shifting values and guidelines that are not dependable, especially during times of decision or stress. Without established life principles, people have no standard to compare their actions and choices to. For many there is no right or wrong, and we see the damage to many people's lives based on this type of thinking. People often do what "seems right" to them. God's Word has something to say about that.

Proverbs 14:12 says, "There is a way that seems right to a man, but in the end it leads to death." This is a shocking reality at times. Things that seem so right can be very bad for us. Sure, we all make little mistakes and bad decisions, but this is pretty heavy. There are things that look good, smell good, feel good and may seem like great deals, but they are actually hurting us in some way.

Most bad decisions don't lead to instant physical death, but they slowly kill small pieces of our emotions, minds, bodies and even our souls. Society often teaches young people that the older generation is out of touch and stupid.

This has caused many people to grow into adulthood without the benefit of the wisdom of the previous generation. Some young people have not had the benefit of the older generation teaching them their true worth and how to live with self-respect and healthy self-esteem.

Overcoming Poverty and/or Victim Mentality

Poverty mentality is usually generational and found in all cultures and backgrounds. I have met people who are convinced that they will always be poor. One of my favorite preachers, Keith Moore, says that a lot of people say, "I am poor but proud." He quickly follows this by saying that "God will deliver you from both." I have heard others say that is OK to be broke but not to be poor. Broke is a temporary situation where you don't have money. Poor is a mindset and a lifestyle.

A season or lifetime of financial struggle can leave a person's heart and self-esteem wounded. There have been a few people who have exaggerated or made it seem easy to get rich after a couple of prayers, and this has caused people to shy away from the fact that God wants to elevate us in our financial situation. God doesn't want to give us money just to have it, but because we need it for ourselves and to do the many good things that He wants us to do to help others.

If we have been stuck in a poverty mindset, I'm not saying that unlimited riches are a prayer away. But I am confidant that God wants to get you unstuck from an unhealthy mindset and on your way to a healthy financial future. It will take hard work, faith and living obediently to God's Word, but first you have to get unstuck in your mindset. Poverty is not God's will for your life.

Other people may have a victim mentality. These people have usually experienced injustice either at an important moment in life or on an ongoing basis. Injustice can be one of the most difficult things to overcome. It is hard to forget because injustice is just flat out wrong and unfair. Injustice is often an act of someone in power harming someone they have the ability to treat badly and get away with the act. This goes against our sense of dignity and attempts to devalue us. It is a direct attack on our soul and spirit. The goal of those who deliberately abuse others or try to keep people down is to somehow keep them in a weakened or damaged state. These wounds can be some of the worst, which makes it even more important to overcome them and not get stuck in their painful reality.

But if we are not careful, we can stay trapped in a place of pain long after the one who hurt us doesn't even care or remember what they did. Even with God in our lives, this type of damage can linger in our lives for years or even decades. In Luke 23:34 Jesus said, "Father, forgive them, for they do not know what they are doing" as the men who crucified Him were rolling dice to see who would get to keep Jesus' clothes as He watched while hanging on the cross! Talk about not getting stuck in the pain of injustice!

The key to healing is not holding onto the pain of past injustice, even if it was deliberate. We need God's help to give grace to others. One of the definitions of grace is forgiving others even when they don't deserve it.

Experiencing God's Grace and Giving It to Others

I used to be a person that never forgave anyone and never asked for forgiveness. I have learned much and grown wiser since then. Jesus died on the cross so that I could be forgiven for all the wrong and even horrible things that I did in my life. This forgiveness became so real to me that I had to forgive others. This is not a fairy tale faith. I have lived it. If you need help, just ask Jesus to help you forgive every injustice you have ever had to live through. Forgiving others is the key to living free ourselves.

Forward Financial Progress and Thinking

I was working with a young man who was in college and did not have a license or car. In fact, no one in his family owned a car. He was also working a part-time job making a little over a hundred dollars a week. After a rather interesting conversation and a little confrontation, I convinced him that not having a license and car was holding him back. I then helped him get a job where he could make the same money in one or two days that he would make in a week. A few months later, he had a license and a car. He is also on his way to become the first college graduate in his family. He grew up in a difficult situation but is well on his way to being an overcomer and very successful in life. He is not letting a family history and mindset keep him from living the great life that God created him to live.

Overcoming Low Self-Esteem

Low self-esteem can be caused by a wounded heart. Some feel that they are ugly or not worthy of love, or don't think they could ever marry someone of high quality. I have seen people go from loser to loser or stay in an emotionally or physically abusive relationship because they think it is better to be with someone who is abusive than to be alone. The problem with this is that people slowly die emotionally in addition to being physically, intellectually and spiritually damaged. They also become unattractive to the kind of person they really should be with.

I have seen others overcome and break this cycle by turning to Jesus and learning over time how much they are truly worth, who God created them to be and the type of life that God has already planned for them. When people learn these things they begin to carry themselves with confidence and no longer compromise on how they let people treat them. This sets the stage where they begin to attract others who are looking for a confident person of high quality and high expectations in life. I have seen both young and old make this change. Unfortunately, I have also seen people repeat the same mistakes over and over again. That's the definition of stuck on stupid and can be difficult to overcome.

Whenever we feel pain in life the natural thing to do is to find what is causing it and make it stop. There are times when we are not sure what the cause is so we blame God. The blame game doesn't get us anywhere in life, but we still need to answer the question: Why does God let bad things happen?

Remember we talked about how God loves us and wants us to love Him? You see, robots don't love, people do. The problem is that you can't create people with the ability to love without making it a choice, and they also have to be able to choose the opposite of love. Since people can choose not to love, they can choose to hurt people. Here is an example of what blaming God for everything can look like.

You Can't Blame the Secretary of Transportation

In the United States there is a Secretary of Transportation who oversees the road system in the country. It is their job to set certain laws and make sure things are done with the transportation system. Is it their fault when someone decides to get drunk, speed and crash into another car causing death and injury? It can't be their fault. He/she may make laws and make sure that people enforce them and punish those who break them, but it is not their fault when a person breaks them. The same thing is true with God. In the Bible He has given us rules, commandments and guidelines to live our life. If we don't take the time to learn them or follow them, it's not His fault is it? God didn't make robots. He made people who could love, give and share; but you can't have that without giving them the choice to hate, steal and be greedy.

So when a person has a wounded heart usually two things happen: It drives them to God for comfort and healing, or it drives them away from God because of the pain. It's funny how sometimes we run away from the thing we need most in life! God also understands what it is like to be rejected by people. How many people use God's name as a curse word? And how did Jesus feel when one of His best friends betrayed Him, another denied even knowing Him and 10 others deserted Him! He understands pain!

Since Jesus understands pain, He understands what you are going through and is ready and able to help you. Jesus said, "I am the light of the world, whoever follows me will never walk in darkness" (John 8:12). The reason people repeat bad decisions, stay in bad situations or continue self-destructive behaviors is because they are "walking in darkness." That darkness includes things like confusion; uncertainty; pride and lack of knowledge, wisdom or understanding. This darkness makes it difficult to see things clearly. As we follow Jesus, He promises to lead us. This applies to all situations in life. Jesus will always lead us in the best direction to make decisions that lead to the best life.

Jesus not only wants to help us get unstuck on stupid, but also to move into the abundant life He promises in John 10:10, which says, "I have come that they may have life, and have it abundantly" (NKJV). In order to enter into the abundant life and stay there, we will be learning how to guard our hearts each and every day.

Chapter 9

Key 6 – Learn to Guard Your Heart

Once we have identified and stopped the action or behavior that wounded us, the next step is learning to guard our heart from further damage. This is necessary so that our wound can actually heal. Remember that God's Word teaches us that the "most important" thing we need to do is guard our hearts. "Above all else, guard your heart" (Proverbs 4:23). This tells me two things. First, there are people and things in our world that will damage our hearts if we let them. Second, guarding our heart may not come naturally to us. If it was an automatic instinct that was important to us, we would not have to be told to do it. If we did it naturally, God would not put a priority on it by saying that we should protect our heart "above all else."

It's not realistic that we will go through life with no pain or disappointments, but I think that we go through a lot more than we need to. Would you rather learn from a little pain or go through a great deal of pain? We do have a choice. There was a commercial a few years back for a mechanic shop that suggested that you come to their business for regular maintenance that would cost a few dollars instead of not taking the precaution and paying a lot more later. The punch line was: "You can pay me now or you can pay me later." Life is a lot like that at times. Sometimes life causes us some pain. If we learn from pain now, it will help us a lot later. If we don't learn from pain now, we will probably learn from a whole lot more pain later!

Pain Is a Great Educator

One of the unfortunate realities of life is that we often will not change or think as deeply about things until the price of pain becomes more than we want to pay. I have heard it said that people won't change until the pain of staying the same is more than the pain of changing. How many people like pain? Not too many, and those that do could use a little psychological help if you know what I mean!

People say that experience is a great teacher. I agree with that statement. I personally have found out that pain is a great educator, too. Most people don't like change. It's just easier to stay the same isn't it? Not always. There are two ways to learn from experience: from other people's situations or your own. Now I believe in experiencing as many *positive* things as you can in life. I also believe that many things that seem negative when they occur can cause very positive changes. I also know that I don't have to get run over by a car to know that I don't want to experience that! We have the ability to learn from the experiences of others instead of having to go through painful things ourselves.

Well, if you're anything like I used to be, you're in for some pain! I used to think I knew everything and wanted to experience everything for myself. A funny thing happened along the way. I found out that the more I learned, the less I actually knew. I found out that sometimes other people were right about things. I also realized that my choices could affect me for years to come. I'm a little bit older and wiser now, but not too old and still growing in wisdom! I guess my point is that many of the things we need to know in life we can learn from others. We can see their pain and hopefully not have to go through it ourselves. This book is all about God healing wounded hearts, but God gives us some great advice. He recommends that we make a huge priority of guarding our heart and protecting it. Will He heal it? Yes, He will, but it's always easier to have and keep something healthy than to go through a long healing process that may still result in long-term or even permanent damage.

An Ounce of Prevention Is Worth a Pound of Cure!

God is very concerned about our well-being and our happiness. He made us with a tremendous ability to feel. You may wonder why God even allows pain. My answer is that He has to! You wouldn't know what hot was unless you could compare it to cold. You wouldn't know that something was bad unless you had something good to compare it to. I think that you are only capable of feeling pleasure to the same degree that you are capable of feeling pain. You can't have one without the other. So does God want us to feel pain? I don't think so, but He has made us with the ability to do so. God also uses pain to teach us things. He doesn't cause it, but allows it. From Proverbs 4:23 we can see what God's advice is about our heart. Guard it! It is actually a command. It is not a suggestion or gentle advice, it is very clear.

If you are anything like me, there are times when you don't like being told what to do! But when God tells us to do something, it is always for our benefit. He knows everything about everything. He loves us so much that He went to the cross to die for us so that we can have an everlasting relationship with Him. I have learned that just about everything and everyone will let me down from time to time, but that God never lets me down. He never disappoints me. He never leads me in the wrong direction. I have learned to say "Yes Sir" to God. He has taught me that He can be trusted. And what is He telling us? He is telling us to guard our heart! But what should we guard it from? We should guard it from anything or anyone that could cause it damage. When people talk about this verse of scripture, many times they just say it means not to fall in love with someone who will treat you badly. It means a whole lot more! It means don't let anyone hurt your heart. It means to have wisdom regarding who you allow to have access to your heart. It also means if you know someone will hurt you, to shield your heart from them. This can be very difficult and confusing, but let's look at a few situations.

Dating in Our Culture

What if someone came up to you and said, "Hi, you're cute, I would like to get to know you so that I can use you sexually, spend all your money and then dump you!" Most people would run away from that one and be proud that they "protected their heart." You may be thinking that nobody would ever say a thing like that. But if you honestly look at the average "dating relationship" in our culture, my quote above is not exaggerated at all. These things happen in both teen and adult years. The only problem is that people don't come out and say it, but their actions do it over time.

God is telling us to protect our hearts at all times. That is why we should get to know people before we give our hearts away. We should watch how people treat others and learn about their past histories, faith and character over time. One of the greatest ways to protect your heart is to watch people. Genuine people are steady over time. We should get to know people in group situations. One of the great problems with dating a person one-on-one is that either person or both can be fake. In an isolated situation, a person can convince you of just about anything and may act very differently than who they really are. Even if people aren't intentionally being fake they often put on their best behavior on a date.

When we give our hearts to someone and they give us their hearts, you don't just get the best things about them, you get all of them! We are all imperfect and we have to be willing to deal with others' imperfections in any long-term relationship. We should not give our hearts away until we know what are getting into. Romantic love and a lifetime relationship are awesome things and God's plan for most of our lives, but if we try to rush it and don't guard our hearts, the results can be devastating. It is always easier to go slowly and take our time than to spend weeks, months and even years picking up the pieces of our broken hearts. God will heal our broken hearts, but it is His plan for us to guard them and avoid being hurt in the first place!

People don't usually rush into good things, if you know what I mean. Usually they rush into the wrong type of things. You will also find that by being cautious, you will find other people who are wisely not in a hurry to be attached to someone. Desperate people often attract other desperate people, and that's a recipe for disaster! One of the problems with our society is that desperate, broken and messed up people have learned to look good. Media glorifies all of the breakups, make-ups and hook-ups going on in Hollywood, and people have come to a place where this is seen as normal. That is another reason why taking your time to get to know someone you're interested in is a wise move. We even need to see people when they are mad and how they react. Unfortunately, I have seen people get fooled until after the wedding bells, and then they find out they married a mad man or crazy woman!

Stomping on the Heart

When I talk about dating with groups of people, I use a very helpful example. I take a red heart cut out of construction paper. I then ask for a very pretty girl to volunteer. There are usually quite a few willing to volunteer! Then I do a little drama thing and say nice things to her and then ask her for her heart. Every time I have done this, the girl has given the heart to me. Then I take the heart and put it on the ground and then proceed to jump up and down on it and stomp it. I then pick it up, give it back to her and tell her I didn't mean it. I say I'm sorry, I love her and then ask for it back. They never give it back when we do the skit and I praise them.

The problem is that in real life many people let others stomp on their heart and then take those same people back or find someone new to stomp on it! You never need to be desperate! God created you in His image with infinite value and worth! Never let anyone treat you badly. Take your time, let God love you and make good friends, the rest will work out in time. As we will see in the next chapter, only God can truly meet the needs of our heart. It is only after we allow God to do His part in our life that all of our other relationships will be fulfilling. Too many times, we try to depend on people who are not dependable and they let us down. Let's be wise and listen to God's advice. Above all else, let's guard our hearts.

Chapter 10

Key 7 – Don't Let the Past Determine Your Future

We're not stuck with repeating mistakes anymore and we've decided not to put up with other people's garbage, so we're getting ready to go somewhere. We've also decided to actively and purposely guard our hearts as we move forward. As we travel ahead, the next step of our journey is to avoid being limited or defined by the past.

God's Word teaches us that "because of the Lord's great love we are not consumed, for his compassions never fail. They are new every morning; great is your faithfulness" (Lamentations 3:22-23). Once we have asked for forgiveness and made a choice to live a Christ-centered life, God is not holding our past against us. If God is not holding our past against us, we shouldn't hold our own past against ourselves!

One of the definitions of mercy and compassion is that God forgives us and helps us even when we don't deserve it. Mercy and compassion are a huge blessing because in times of pain we sometimes need help. Mercy means that God overlooks our weaknesses, faults and poor decisions. If we can't get past the pain on our own, God will help us. The reality is that in order to have a great future, we can't let our past or current painful reality define who we really are.

Don't Let the Past Define You

We all have defining moments, relationships and experiences in life. These three aspects of life often mold our thinking and actions. The funny thing is that most great people have experienced both wonderful victories and terrible failures in life. The difference between people who achieve great things and the guy sitting on the bar stool complaining and blaming everyone else for his lousy life is how they react to life's wins, losses and hard times.

Allowing Pain and Failure to Motivate You

Following the 9/11 attack on the Twin Towers many people lost their jobs that day or soon after. Some used this horrible time to refocus on their families, their faith and their own development. Others got discouraged and depressed, and still haven't recovered almost seven years later. I've seen people who have lost houses and families try to drown their sorrows in alcohol. These people all experienced the same tragedy, but reacted differently and experienced very different results. Everyday we have a choice of what we will do with that day. We can stay stuck or move forward. Moving forward is often painful but not as painful as staying in a place of pain or defeat.

Avoiding the Trap of Bitterness

God's Word is clear that we need to be careful that bitterness doesn't become an ongoing part of our lives. "See to it that no one misses the grace of God and that no bitter root grows up to cause trouble and defile many" (Hebrews

12:15). Bitterness can grow like a deep-rooted weed. If you want to get rid of a weed, you have to either kill it with weed killer or literally dig out the entire root. God wants to kill any bitterness you are holding onto with His love, compassion and healing power, as well as literally ripping it out of your life forever. Just like any ugly weed can keep coming back and ruin a beautiful lawn, bitterness will keep coming back and spread itself until it ruins the beautiful life that God has planned for you.

Living the Overcoming Lifestyle

Jesus is the great overcomer! In His life on earth, He helped people overcome low self-esteem, weakness, failure, sin, sickness and even death. He overcame sin on the cross and death after three days in the grave. He wants to teach you to overcome the issues you are facing also. One of the things that I love about God is that He doesn't hide reality from us, He teaches us to flourish in the midst of it. Jesus declares to us that we will have trouble to face and overcome. John 16:33 says, "I have told you these things, so that in me you may have peace. In this world you will have trouble. But take heart! I have overcome the world."

I often joke that this is the one promise that Jesus makes that I don't like. Jesus never promises to remove every trouble from our lives, but He does tell us that we don't have to worry about life's troubles, we just have to overcome them. Followers of Christ, over time, are supposed to become like Jesus and do the things that He did. If He was an overcomer, then we, too, should become more like Him as we overcome both small and big things in life. The key to becoming this type of overcomer is learning from the greatest overcomer Himself.

The Power of Following Christ

Almost all people believe in some type of "god," whether or not they go to church on a regular basis. However, many of these people, if they were asked if God was working powerfully in their lives would either say "no" or look at you kind of weird. The power is not in believing in some type of generic god out there or regularly attending a church service or some other type of spiritual pursuit. Walking in "overcomer power" is also much different than just being forgiven of sin. This is a step towards power, but becoming an overcomer is a different process. There are a lot of people who have been forgiven of their sins but who have not yet learned to walk in the resurrection power of Jesus Christ! If God the Father can raise Jesus from the dead through the power of the Holy Spirit, He can help us overcome the little issues we face each day!

In order to experience this type of power, we have to follow Jesus in obedience. This may not appeal to our intellect at first because we often have a negative opinion of authoritative religious people because of the ways some have acted in the past. I am not talking about complete obedience to an imperfect person or religious organization. I am talking about obedience to Jesus who is God and loves us so much that He literally died for us so that we could be forgiven and spend eternity with Him in heaven.

I was asked to speak at a church called Greater Grace Fellowship in Newark, N.J., as part of a conference they were holding. I began to pray and ask God what I should speak about and the word that came to my mind was "obedience." My first thought was, "I'm not so sure people want to hear about obedience on Friday night of a conference." I later asked what the theme of the conference was and the pastor told me "Livin' the Good Life." I thought, "Isn't that great. God tells me to speak about obedience when the crowd wants to hear about living good lives." I laughed as I thought about whether or not I was going to be obedient myself.

After I got done laughing at myself and God's sense of humor, I began to think about it. If we want to live the good life that God has created for us to live, it absolutely requires obedience. It took a few minutes to break it down, but the crowd began to receive the message and later the pastor told me it was exactly what the people needed to hear. Following Jesus in obedience even if we don't understand all the details, unleashes overcoming power.

If you could overcome life's struggles through your own wisdom and strength, you would have already overcome them and you wouldn't be reading this book right now. Some of the keys to walking in God's power are humility, obedience and relying on His strength, wisdom and power as He teaches us. Jesus wants to lead you. The only question is "will you follow?"

Chapter 11

Key 8 – Let God Direct Your Life

As we go through life each day, many people influence our choices and decisions. Advertisers spend millions of dollars trying to direct people to their products and people listen, otherwise they wouldn't spend that money. Infomercials are on TV and radio because people are influenced by them. Some people proudly boast that no one influences them and that they make their own choices in all things. First, this is not true, and second, God warns against making all of your decisions based on your own knowledge and understanding. "Trust in the Lord with all your heart and lean not on your own understanding" (Proverbs 3:5).

God is teaching us that no matter how smart we are, we won't get it right if we don't lean on Him and allow Him to direct us. The reason so many of us are walking around with wounded hearts is because we trusted in people or things with our heart instead of the Lord.

We are all looking for happiness and a good life. But very few people find it. Psalm 37:4 is a recipe for happiness in our lives: "Delight yourself in the Lord and he will give you the desires of your heart." God is the supplier of all good things. In the Old Testament, one of the names that God uses to describe Himself is El Shaddai, which means "the God who is more than enough." This literally means that He has more than we could ever use; more things, more happiness, more joy than we can even think or imagine. The problem many of us have is that we spend all of our time and energy going after the things we want instead of going directly to the supplier who can give them to us—and much, much more! When we put God first in our lives, He promises to take care of the rest. God is the source of the things that will make us happy in our lives. A major step in healing and avoiding a wounded heart is having our needs met. As God meets our need to be loved, we can heal. As God meets our needs, we won't chase after people to meet them. God also promises to give us a peace that is greater than we can even understand (see Philippians 4:7). When we have this peace, we will choose from the best instead of just choosing from what is available at that time.

Many people have trouble trusting a God they can't see. But what is even more amazing is that so many people trust people and things that they know they can't depend on. So many people are willing to trust individuals who have a track record of doing wrong things instead of trusting God! People expect imperfect and even evil people to make them happy! One of the greatest things that God does when you trust Him is to change your desires. God will change you to desire the things that you really need and can really trust. I have seen it in my life and the lives of so many people over the years. He will do it in your life too. How do I know? I know because God does not change and He considers all people equal. So anything He does for other people, He will do for you, too!

Have You Ever Seen the Wind?

Some people who are still learning to recognize the presence of God and how He wants to be part of their lives often feel that since they can't see God, He isn't real. Here is my question: Have you ever seen the wind? Obviously, you can't see wind. People will say that you can, but it is impossible. Wind is invisible. But people will say, "Yeah, but you can see what the wind does." The same is true for God. You can't see Him, but you can see all of the things that He does! If the wind is powerful, how much more powerful is the One who made it?

God is Our Source

When you want a new car where do you go? You go to the car dealer. You can't get a new car from the Dairy Queen! You may be able to get some good ice cream, but they don't have cars. God says He will give you the desires of your heart when you put Him first in your life and enjoy Him! The "desires of your heart" sure covers a lot of territory. Remember we are talking about the God who is "more than enough." When we come to truly understand this and live it, it sure takes off a lot of the pressure in life.

God Loves His Children

Why would God want to do so many nice things for us? He does them because He loves us and because He can't not love us! He is love and can do nothing else but love us. Over the years I have been amazed by some parents' love for their children. I have met parents whose kids seemed like the most unlovable people you could ever meet, but when you sat down and talked about their kids, they would talk about them with such true love that it would amaze you. If people can love other people so much, just imagine how much God is able to love us. We don't have to wonder if He loves us, He does. The only time we don't feel God's love is when we reject it! You may be saying right now that you can't feel it. Take a moment and ask God to teach you how much He loves you. Spend time each day talking to Him and you will begin to understand when you seek Him. He promises that He will be found! He promises that if you draw near to Him, that He will draw near to you (see James 4:8). Try it and you will see for yourself.

Allowing God to be your provider in all things is a recipe for success. Over the years I've learned that I can not get all the things that I need or want on my own. I've also learned that people cannot give me all that I need or want. There have also been many times that God has opened doors that I could never have opened myself.

Let God Direct You into the Plan He Already Has For Your Life

We often strive with everything we have to succeed or achieve the things that we think will bring us fulfillment and happiness. We map out a game plan for our lives but often come to the reality that our plan is a lot better on paper or in our mind than in reality. God already has the best plan for our lives. Instead of trying to come up with a better one, we should spend our time and energy connecting with Him so that we can recognize His leading and follow. This type of direction only comes through a deep, personal relationship with Jesus. We may have to be willing to move past some things in order to move onto the path that He has for us.

Chapter 12

Key 9 – Let Go!

Here are two words that will change your life: "Let go!" I was in a worship service a couple of years ago and God gave me a vision of someone in the church. In this vision they were holding onto the past while reaching towards their future. Their face expressed great straining, pain and frustration because they were holding onto their past. A better future was literally inches away, but they could not bring themselves to a place of letting go. The reality was that this person had been abused. As a result, they experienced a lot of pain, low self-esteem and an inability to move forward in life. God had something better for them but they would never get it unless they let go of the past. What is it that you are holding onto that God wants you to let go? If you want to move forward and overcome the pain and disappointment, you must let go. Even when you are not sure what lies ahead, you have to let go. You will never find out unless you do.

When I was a high school teacher, I was in charge of a program called Project Adventure. This was a program where we did a lot of team building exercises that required trust. One of the activities involved blindfolding a person and their partner had to guide them without touching them. Some people enjoyed this while others just could not trust someone when they could not see where they were going. Sometimes our faith in the Lord is like Project Adventure. We have to trust God even when we can't see where He is leading us. The person with the best partner would get to the end of the path the quickest, safest way and had a great time. When we allow God to lead us, we have a partner who knows and sees everything and will always lead us in the right direction—even when we can't see it's the best way!

Remember Proverbs 3:5-6, "Trust in the Lord with all your heart and lean not on your own understanding; in all your ways acknowledge him and he will make your paths straight." We all put our trust into someone or something. It is amazing what some people will trust for their happiness and with their heart. This verse teaches us to trust in the Lord above everything else, even ourselves! God is teaching us that He knows the way better than us. When we allow Him to guide us through life, He will always lead us the right way; the Bible calls it the straight path. This means that we can avoid the traps and detours in our life, and we'll make the best progress to happiness, great relationships and living life to the fullest!

It is amazing that people will listen to almost any so-called expert from TV or in the magazines even when they give crazy advice. Have you ever been in the car with a driver who is lost and refuses to stop and ask for directions or buy a map? I once heard of a story where a truck driver drove eight hours in the wrong direction before he asked for directions. That sounds crazy, but that's how many people live their lives. God has given us the Bible, which can be a guidebook for life if we will just open it up for directions. He also gives us the Holy Spirit to guide us into all truth if we will just slow down enough to ask for directions. Otherwise we are just like that truck driver who was too stubborn to ask for directions and we waste a whole lot of time, energy and money going in the wrong direction.

There have been other times when I have been driving and don't know where I am going but there is a passenger who knows the way. My wife has a photographic memory for directions. She can remember where to turn from a trip she made years ago. It amazes me. It amazes me even more when I trust God and He directs me when I'm not sure where I am going. I have learned that even if I don't see or understand everything, He does.

Let Go and Let God

When we hold on to things it is because we are trying to fix our own problems. When we do that we are basically telling God that we can handle it and don't need Him to help us. Since God has given us a free will to make choices in life, He respects our decision to handle it ourselves. The reality is that we can use all the help we can get. When we intentionally let go of something we can then invite God to enter into the situation and begin to change it, transform our minds and heal our wounds. These are the times when we learn how to experience the power and presence of God in our daily lives. It is also what He wants to do. My prayer is that you choose today by your free will to let go of that painful thing and let God come into your situation. I have also learned that when I follow His direction in my life, I learn a whole lot of things along the way.

One of the keys to letting go is learning to trust people once again. I'm not saying we should just trust anyone; that would be foolish. Hopefully, we are all growing wiser as the days pass. It is always good to surround yourself with people who care about you and who are committed to loving and protecting you. For some, this may seem like a fairy tale at this point, but it does not have to be. In fact, part of healing past wounds and protecting against future wounds is being surrounded by good people.

Chapter 13

Key 10 – Build a Winning Team

Winning teams don't just happen. They are built. There is a boss or head coach that orchestrates the team-building process. You have to be the one who purposely builds a winning team to help you win in life. Many people go through life without ever thinking about the importance of surrounding themselves with as many great people as possible. I have also met individuals who think they can make it without the help of others.

There is a saying that "the banana that is away from the bunch is the first one to get peeled." This saying is letting us know that we are safer when we are surrounded by others than when we are by ourselves. The reason that fish swim in schools is that they are less likely to be eaten when they are with others. In the same way, it is wise to surround ourselves with family, friends and church members who love us and are there to help us. Even the Lone Ranger had Tonto! The Bible also teaches us that we will have victory when we have many wise counselors: "Plans fail for lack of counsel, but with many advisers they succeed" (Proverbs 15:22).

Recently, I was watching a nature show that talked about how lions and other predators focus on the young, weak, sick, old and those that have been pulled away from the herd. God's Word describes Satan, the enemy of our souls, as a roaring lion looking around to see who he can devour. "Be self-controlled and alert. Your enemy the devil prowls around like a roaring lion looking for someone to devour" (1 Peter 5:8). So if you are spiritually immature, hurt, confused or alone, you are a good target for Satan. In the wild even the strongest animals stay in herds. They do this for personal protection and to protect others. Our human "herds" are our families, our churches and our circle of friends. The stronger those around you are, the more you can overcome and the less you will have to overcome in the days ahead!

We live in a society where having strong families and long-lasting relationships are getting rarer. Communities aren't close-knit like they used to be, and most of us don't know our neighbors or even their names! In my life, in a 12-year span, I graduated from high school, went to college in another part of the state, went to graduate school in another state, moved back to my home state and switched jobs two times. With each move or job change, I left behind most or all of the people I associated with and started all over again. I also lost contact with most of the people who had become my good friends. I was very much alone most of the time without clear direction or the support and guidance of others. This is why even as society seems to continue to speed up and change, there is an even greater need to be connected in a meaningful way with other people. My life has settled down and become more stable, but my story demonstrates how easy it can be to go through life and not have the type of relationships that we need and that are healthy for us to have.

We all have a desire to give our heart to someone. Giving it to the right one will result in happiness and joy. Giving it to the wrong one is a recipe for disaster! There is something powerful about surrendering our heart to someone. Don't believe me? Just look around. The world is trying so hard to give their hearts away to the right one, to the one we can trust. Here is the million dollar question: "Who can we trust?"

Jesus said, "Do not let your hearts be troubled. Trust in God, trust also in me" (John 14:1). Jesus is promising us that we can trust Him. We are looking for that right someone. Jesus is that someone. We are all looking for someone to love and to love us. Jesus demonstrated His love for us by dying for our sins. In fact He said, "Greater love has no one than this, that he lay down his life for his friends" (John 15:13). Many people don't understand why Jesus had to die on a cross. God is a holy God and a just God. He gave us a standard to live by. But we have failed to live up to that standard by sinning. We sin when we go in the opposite direction of God by doing things our way instead of His. There is a judgment or punishment for this and it is eternal separation from God. But God the Father had a plan. He sent Jesus to pay the price in our place. Jesus paid the death penalty for our sins so that we could spend eternity in heaven with God.

Who Are You Trusting for Eternity?

We often spend much time and energy looking for someone we can give our hearts to and trust. Jesus is telling us that we don't have to be troubled. That means we don't have to be confused or stressed out because we can trust Jesus. He will never break your heart, and you can depend on Him at all times. Not only that, but He will guide you in all situations and direct you the right way. Once you have this relationship set, all the others will fall in place. If you have not already begun this most important relationship in your life you can do it now with a simple but powerful prayer:

Dear Jesus, I want to know You. I have sinned against You and am sorry. Thank You for dying on the cross to pay for my sins. Come into my heart, forgive my sins. I am trusting You for all eternity. Today I choose to follow You and put You in charge of my life. Guide me in all that I do and help me to know Your love and plan for my life. I pray this in Your name, Jesus. Amen.

If you just prayed to receive Jesus into your heart as Lord and Savior, congratulations! You just did the greatest thing you could ever do. You just began the most important relationship in your life! Just like any other relationship, the more time you invest in it the more it will grow. Jesus will fill many of those desires in your heart. He also will teach you all about true love. This will give you a guide to measure all of your other relationships. When you begin this relationship, you open your heart so that He can heal it from past hurts. I have experienced this myself.

Then comes something else that is really exciting, He teaches us how to love others. In my life, I never understood love until I received Jesus as my Lord and Savior and He taught me what true love was. Before that, love was just a feeling to me that came and went. But true love doesn't come and go. It lasts, and that is the type of love that we are all looking for. The love of Jesus will give you greater stability in your life than you thought you could ever have. This allows you to have stable relationships in all other areas of your life. This protects your heart in so many ways. Remember that God can and will heal your heart, but His best plan is for you to live in love and wholeness that can only be fully realized through Him.

You Are on Your Way

We have talked about your heart, and how God can heal it. We also talked about protecting it and allowing God to be your first love. You may still be feeling some pain. Give it over to God. Ask Him to heal it. He will. He is the Healer. He is our heavenly Father. He is One who you can trust and He is one you can share with others. Let God into your heart, spend time with Him each day and in the days to come you, too, will be able to declare: "God heals broken hearts!"

Building the Winning Team

The winning team needs to be both spiritual and natural. Many people are so focused on the natural relationships with family, friends and business connections that they neglect their most important relationship with God Himself. The reality is that we need to surround ourselves with good people, but we need God to help us the most in our lives and in these other relationships as well. Other people are so focused on God and think that they don't need to build strong relationships with people, but that is also not wise. Part of the benefits of having a relationship with Jesus is that His blessings, guidance and power will also help us in our natural relationships.

Relationship with Jesus, Your Head Coach

Jesus is all about relationship. "Jesus went up on a mountainside and called to him those he wanted, and they came to him. He appointed twelve—designating them apostles—that they might be with him and that he might send them out to preach" (Mark 3:13-14). When Jesus chose a group of uneducated and unimpressive men to be His followers, He knew the great things that they needed to do. The secret to doing great things is not just education or going to church or being really smart, it's developing the character of Jesus. He didn't expect people to become more like Him simply by going to church or knowing about Him. He knew that in order for us to be transformed and changed, we must spend time with Him. Unfortunately, most people think that means just going to church and trying to be a good person. We should do these things, but that is a small part of having a relationship with Jesus. He not only wants to be with us, but also to lead us the right way in all of the complicated situations that we face in life.

In John 8:12 He says, "I am the light of the world. Whoever follows me will never walk in darkness but will have the light of life." This is not only talking about eternity, but walking out our lives day by day. "Whoever" is one of my favorite words in the Bible because I fit the qualifications and so do you. The prerequisite to living a life where we can see and understand what is best for us is not being brilliant, successful or having the right earthly connections, but being willing to follow Jesus. Whether your life has been pretty good or a living nightmare, you qualify to have Jesus personally help you each and every day. Many people only reach out for Jesus' help after tragedy has struck. Because He loves us so much He is there for us at those times, but wouldn't it be much better to reach out to Him each day so that we can avoid the train wrecks of life instead of asking Him to heal us afterwards? He wants to be on our team, but we have to choose to follow Him so that we can be on His.

Holy Spirit, Your Personal Coach

In sports, there are many coaches. In baseball, there are base coaches that watch where the ball is on the field and tell the runner to either stop at the base or keep running. In basketball and football, the coaches are always yelling instructions to the players on how to react to the current situation and discussing past and upcoming situations in the game during time outs and half-time breaks. If grown men and women need coaches to help them win a game, don't we need a great coach to win life? God's Word teaches us that "those who are led by the Spirit of God are sons of God" (Romans 8:14). The word "sons" when literally translated means "maturing ones." This means that those of us who are maturing in our relationship with Christ will be led by the Holy Spirit. And the more we mature spiritually, the more we will be led by the Holy Spirit.

In the same way that sports coaches are more knowledgeable as an athlete proceeds through grammar school, high school, college and into the professional ranks, as we mature in our faith we get greater coaching from the Holy Spirit. In the same way that a 10 year old would not be able to receive college level coaching, spiritually immature people are not ready for the type of guidance God really wants to give them. That is why ongoing spiritual growth is so necessary.

Many people spend their entire lives in church but don't receive the guidance God wants to give them. That's because they have not purposely chosen to spend time with God and discipline themselves to have a life of prayer and Bible study. God has all the direction we need. We just have to put ourselves in the position to receive it. The Holy Spirit is ready to guide us in the midst of everyday life. He also wants us to take some time-outs to receive advice and direction before we head back into the game of life. In sports, time-outs are often taken at the most important time or when there is a momentum shift for the other side. It's just common sense then that during life's most important situations or when our lives look like they may be taking a turn in the wrong direction, that we call a time-out and get with God. The difference is that it will probably take longer than a 30-second time-out to get all the direction we need. My advice is to take all the time you need with God, be patient and it will be worth it in life.

The Importance of a Church Family

The Church is not a building. It is the people who have made a choice to follow Jesus Christ. While there are many church buildings, in God's view there is only one "Church." This is not based on what man has established, but on what God has established. What makes a person a member of God's church family is repenting from sin, putting all of their hope in the forgiveness of sin through the shedding of Jesus' very own blood during the crucifixion and submission to the Lordship of Jesus Christ. God established the Church for a couple of purposes. Community and friendship are two of the main purposes. The original words for "church" in the Bible literally meant a group of individuals who had no purpose and were given an individual purpose at the same time, connecting them with others for a purpose greater than themselves. There are many benefits to having a church family in addition to connecting with people who may share your faith but attend another church. Here is God's advice to us:

> And let us consider how we may spur one another on toward love and good deeds. Let us not give up meeting together, as some are in the habit of doing, but let us encourage one another—and all the more as you see the Day approaching. (Hebrews 10:24-25)

These two verses, give us some great direction. First, we must purposely think about how we can encourage people to love one another and do good things for others. This lets me know that I may not demonstrate love and good deeds without the encouragement of others. Second, is that we need to purposely meet together. I've found out that if I don't purposely schedule times to get together with people, it won't happen. It is actually easy to get in the habit of not getting together, even with people that we want to be with! But it is easy to do even in bad times. We must make sure that we don't get so preoccupied with life and its challenges that we don't spend the time we need with others to receive the very encouragement we need to keep going.

Our Family is Part of our Support Team

For some, family is the most important thing in life. For others, it is not a priority. For many, family is important but the responsibilities of life can be overwhelming. I have seen studies where they attach microphones to small children and the average time that some fathers spend talking to their children is less than two minutes a day! Many people have also grown up in broken families or been raised by single parents and may have no idea of what healthy family life actually is. Whatever your situation, I encourage you to build your family in whatever ways that you can. You will be happy you did.

Friends – Finishing Off Our Team

We need good friends for many reasons: for support, encouragement, acceptance and just to have fun! Friends can supply a listening ear, loving advice and stability over time. We also often do the things our friends do. This is why it is important to have friends that have great values and goals in life. We will either soar like eagles or wallow through the mud with our friends. Choose your friends wisely.

God built us for relationship with Him and with people. We need both. God has a great destiny for us, but we need a team around us that will help us reach that destiny. Life has risks and challenges. The greater the team we surround ourselves with, the more positive risks we will be willing to take and the greater challenges we will be able to overcome.

Chapter 14

Key 11 – Be a Positive Risk Taker

Too many people live timid lives. They have been hurt and want to make sure that it doesn't happen again. My experience is that many people who have gone through hard times or faced difficult situations will do the minimum to get by and get on with life. Past disappointment can make us fearful of taking risks or cause us not to try our hardest because of the possibility that there will be no benefit or reward at the end of the day.

I love success and don't like failure; whether this has been in school, on the job, in relationships or just around the house. I have had several relationships in my life with people that I couldn't please. I tend not to be detail-oriented or a perfectionist in how I do things. I'm a big picture kind of guy. I may be a little messy but it will get done. If I spend too much time around detail-oriented people, I get frustrated and begin to shut down or disengage emotionally. The more disengaged I get, the less motivated I am and less I care or try. If not careful, these relationships get more and more stressful and less productive. I have had to learn how to communicate better and reach agreement with these types of people.

You may be emotionally shut down from the ongoing conflict or overwhelming criticism. I have had to teach myself to let go of these frustrations and pains and stir up my passion for life or for a particular job, project or even relationship. Whether it has been a traumatic event that has hurt you or the day-to-day conflict or stress, we have to learn to let go so that we can live happy, productive lives.

Pain, failure and disillusionment can have a paralyzing effect. God has much more planned for your life. Jesus said in John 10:10, AMP, "I came that they may have and enjoy life, and have it in abundance (to the full, till it overflows)".

God doesn't just want to heal you. He wants to make you whole, live in confidence and begin to take wise positive risks. Nobody ever achieves greatness without taking a risk. No one ever gets a new job or promotion or begins a new relationship without taking a risk. In fact if we want to achieve and experience the greatest things in life, we have to be progressively greater risk takers.

Proper Risk Taking Requires Wisdom

You may have taken risks in the past and you gotten burned pretty bad. Many people take risks, but quite honestly, some of them were pretty bad decisions that have been very costly. These are not the type of risks I am talking about. I am talking about living by the standard of God's Word and being led by the Holy Spirit. God will direct us to a place of destiny that may seem impossible without Him but you know that He wants you to take the risk. In fact, you can not achieve greatness and live out your life's purpose without taking great risks. The important thing is that if you are following Jesus and He is leading you, what may seem like a great risk in the natural is actually meant to be an exciting adventure in the natural and spiritual realms.

Risk Taking is a Necessity

God created you to live an exciting and powerful life. He created each of us with a purpose, and living out your individual purpose will be the most fun, most fulfilling life you could live. Many people never live out this purpose because they stay stuck in the past. Satan also wants to keep us in a static position. He wants to remind you of pain and failure, and fill you with fear to keep you stuck in your past. Satan wants to convince you that you can't change or grow or be healed. Those are all lies.

Overcoming the Enemy of Fear

Fear is your enemy. It will paralyze you and hold you back your entire life if you let it. Fear is not just an emotion, it is actually a spiritual thing. In 2 Timothy 1:7 it says, "For God hath not given us a spirit of fear; but of power, and of love and of a sound mind" (KJV).

Fear is a spiritual issue and it is not God's will for your life. The Spirit that God gives us results in power, love and self-discipline. This means the more you invite Jesus into your life, and allow Him to lead you in every area, the more you will experience power, love and self-discipline. God's Word also says, "There is no fear in love. But perfect love drives out fear, because fear has to do with punishment" (1 John 4:18).

This means that the more we grow and experience God's love in our lives, the love of God "drives out fear". You can stand up against fear and begin to walk in peace and confidence. Taking risks will no longer be scary. It may be uncomfortable to take risks but it will not be fearful. You will also learn to give yourself freedom to succeed. You will also open up the opportunity for failure, but it will be greatly reduced and you won't put yourself into a position where you will experience devastating failure.

Examples of God-Led Risk Taking

I began working in a local church with teens. I still remember putting together a mailing list of 68 teens. I thought we were big stuff! 10 years later we have almost 1,000 teens that go to our church. Along the way, we took a lot of risks. We started a choir with teens who could barely sing. They have sung all over New York and New Jersey, including in front of 13,000 people in Madison Square Garden, and at the Izod Center in the Meadowlands in New Jersey. Our dance team, which consists of untrained teens who have been taught to be worshippers, has traveled as far as Malaysia and South Africa for dance conferences. These were all great risks.

I knew God was leading me to write books. I started this book in 2004 and finished it in 2008. Along the way were a lot of smaller risks, hard work and a good deal of rejection from publishing companies and author agents. In their world I was unproven and too risky. There were times when I had to ignore rejections, overcome pain and frustration, stir up the passion and keep going. I live in a place of constant risk that is truly an adventure. The fact that you are reading this is proof that it does makes a difference each time we refuse to quit in life and choose to chase after our dreams.

When it comes to relationships there were several years after I began my relationship with God that I didn't go on any dates. I had to go through a healing process. I had to grow in wisdom. I knew I wasn't ready. The time came when I felt ready and I asked God to clearly show me who I should marry because I did not trust my own judgment. My wife and I are going on our seventh year of marriage. It hasn't always been easy, but it has been worth it. I took the risk after the healing of my heart while constantly seeking God's wisdom. There has been some pain, healing and risk taking even within the marriage. These things are part of life. We can try to avoid them but all that does is put us in a box where we can't really live life. It may be safer, but it's not living.

Chapter 15

Key 12 – Live a Great Life!

So now it's time to live! Jeremiah 29:11 says, " 'For I know the plans I have for you,' declares the LORD, 'plans to prosper you and not to harm you, plans to give you hope and a future.' " Just as God spoke to Jeremiah about having a plan for Him, God also has plans for us as individuals. His Word teaches us that before we were born, He knew us. Living a great life is not accomplished through our own planning, but through walking out the plan that God already has for us. The issue is that if we want to know the best plans we could ever live, we have to go to God. He reveals these plans to us through His Word and through the guidance of the Holy Spirit. God has already established these plans, but it is just up to us to live them out.

God's plans are always good for us and never meant to hurt us. Prosperity in the many different areas of life demonstrates that we are following God's plans. Most of the pain in our lives demonstrates that we are out of God's will and trying to live out our own plan. Even if we experience pain along with God's plan, in the end it will be worth it because of the greater benefit of what God wants to achieve. God even uses times of trial to make us stronger, have greater faith and build character, which leaves us better off in the long run.

As we learn that God has a plan for us and we begin to live it out, it will give us hope. So many people are living without hope. Every time a person gets drunk or high, it is a demonstration of a lack of hope. They put their hope in a bottle or a pill that may numb the pain and provide some pleasure, but not a better tomorrow. Even if we have chosen the wrong path in life, we can get on the right path at any moment. It may not erase all the damage of yesterday, but it can get us going in the right direction. Hope means that no matter what life looks like at this moment, it can be better tomorrow. To many people this seems more like a dream than reality. But God's reality is that He has the hope-giving plan ready for us, we just have to get with His program.

God's plans also let us know that we have a good future ahead of us. I have met so many people who are striving for a better future. While I agree that we should all be striving for our futures, it is best to strive for the future that God wants for us. Whatever man can earn, man can lose. Whatever we can create or build will eventually break down or fall apart. When God establishes something, there is nothing that can change it. That's the kind of future I want: one that will not fall apart over time.

We were not created to live average or boring lives, and surely not the sad and even tragic lives that we see people living. We were created to live abundantly good lives, but it is a choice. I've taken groups of teens to amusement parks. Once they get there, they break into groups and go to the different rides and areas of the park. At the end of the day we meet up to go home. I often ask different kids and groups how their day went. It's funny hearing the different responses that I get. One group will be filled with joy and laughter as they talk about the great day and the things they did. Another group will complain about the long lines, rude people and expensive food. I have been told by a few that they didn't enjoy anything. The funny thing about this is that both groups were in the same exact place. The same rides, the same crowds and the same opportunities were available to everyone. One group had a great time and the other group was a bunch of miserable grouches at the end of the day! All of these teens were smart, intelligent and good people. Different choices resulted in totally different experiences. We all have so many great opportunities available to us but we will have to take some risks. How many people do you know walking around complaining about life instead of living it?

    You can live a great life, but you will have to go for it. It is a choice and it is a risk, but it is better than living a lukewarm, boring life. Once you have made the right choices, grown in wisdom and surrounded yourself with a winning team, it is now time to live. God never promises you a perfect life, but He promises you a very good one! Be encouraged. The plan has already been made. It's time to live it out.

Chapter 16

Our Final Goal: Helping Others

One of the greatest steps to healing and freedom in my life was taken when I realized that life wasn't all about me. In fact, a lot of my personal pain was caused by my own selfishness. Many people in our society are too focused on themselves. Many people spend all of their time trying to get ahead or get over on people, while others are too self-consumed with their personal issues to care about anyone else. We talked earlier about walking in God's power. I would like to take a minute to talk about being God-focused. If you have committed to being a follower of Jesus, then you are obligated to live as He lived, or at a minimum to ask God to help you learn how to do that in a greater way over time. God does not give you power just for power's sake, but because He wants you to help others with that power.

I am the founder and president of Fourth Generation Ministries. Our vision statement is very simple: "Receive. Grow. Give it away...." In a nutshell, when we are in the wounded heart discussion mode, we have to receive healing from Jesus. Then, we have to grow in that healing over time. The final step is coming to a place of gratefulness for what God has done in our lives. At that time we can give away the very things that have helped us. Along the way to our healing, we have gotten wiser, learned how to guard our heart, stopped making bad choices and surrounded ourselves with good people. These are valuable things that we all need. What has become normal to you over time will be life changing to those you share it with.

Having the Same Focus as Jesus

Jesus did not walk around trying to figure out what He could get from others, He walked around trying to see how He could help others or share what He already had. I have heard people say that "love is not love until it is given away." I think that has a lot of truth to it. I think also that "someone is not truly healed until they are able to help others move towards healing."

Don't Wait Until You Are 100% Healed

The reality is that healing is a process that takes time, and for some it may be years. Do not wait until you have overcome all things. In fact I have learned that a lot of overcoming and healing takes place while you help others. Many times, God moves most powerfully in our lives when we are focused on others instead of ourselves. Even in times of pain and confusion Jesus was very clear about where His focus was: "Yet not as I will, but as you will" (Matthew 26:39). Even in His toughest moment on the way to being crucified, Jesus was focused on being obedient to the Father's will.

Comforting Others

One of the greatest joys in life is when we are able to help others. God has created us with a need to help people. I have seen some of the roughest, meanest people instantly turn into humble and kind people when presented with the opportunity to help someone who was hurting. Whatever plan God has for your life, along the way, He will put people in your path that need some help. God is very compassionate toward us and He wants us to give this compassion to others:

> Praise be to the God and Father of our Lord Jesus Christ, the Father of compassion and the God of all comfort, who comforts us in all our troubles, so that we can comfort those in any trouble with the comfort we ourselves have received from God. (2 Corinthians 1:3-4)

I learned what this scripture meant on 9/11. I had been on staff for a little over a year at Christ Church in Montclair, N.J., when the terrorist attack took place. Montclair is located in northern New Jersey, west of Manhattan. Many of the people in our community, our friends and their family members worked in New York City and even in the Twin Towers. We have a historic Cathedral in a central location in Montclair in the downtown business area. Our doors were open all day and we had a nonstop prayer meeting for the entire day as we tried to understand what happened and were in the process of locating friends, several of our pastors and many relatives of our congregants and community.

People we had never seen were coming into our church to pray, talk or just to have a shoulder to cry on. Someone actually called our church and said, "I'm an atheist and I don't believe in God, but can I come to your church and just sit?" The reality is that there is something deep within us that knows that we need God. It may only come out during difficult times for some, but it is there. It's moments like these when you realize how inadequate we are in our own strength. God's Word teaches us very clearly what to do. Basically it says that however we have received comfort, we should turn around and comfort others. Even in situations when we don't know exactly what to do, we can be there, be supportive, share what we can and remember that when we come to the end of ourselves, God is just getting started.

I share this story with you to show that you may not be prepared for certain situations. It's not about knowing all the right answers or you being totally healed. It is a matter of being willing to allow God to work through you to help others. One of the worst days of my life became a life changing moment. In the midst of fear, confusion and uncertainty, God was teaching me. He was not the cause of the tragedy, but He was the way through it. He used a terrible reality to change my heart and that has resulted in a more caring and giving heart that continues to help people every day.

God wants to be a blessing for you and those you connect with each day. Even if you are not fully where you want to be, keep going. I've discovered that if people don't quit, God makes a way. He has planned your healing so make sure that you receive it. We have to grow in that healing until it touches every inch of our lives and saturates our soul. After you have earned your degree in pain and healing, you will be a valuable resource to the rest of the world. It is now time to take what we have learned and share it with others. I thank God that He is healing you. Now He wants you to take the next step. You have received many great things so it is now time to give them away.

Our world is filled with people living each day with wounded hearts. Continue walking in the hope and healing power of Jesus Christ. Along the bumpy road of life, Jesus will never leave you. He understands pain and has overcome it. In the days ahead He wants to help you become a great overcomer. "In this world you will have trouble. But take heart! I have overcome the world" (John 16:33).

Hang in there. Let Jesus heal and build you up, and along the way keep your eyes open for those around you. Expect God to bring hurting people into your path because

God wants to heal their wounded hearts also. Never stop and never quit because God is faithful. The days are coming when the pain of today will be a distant memory.

Fourth Generation Ministries

Jack Redmond is the founder and president of Fourth Generation Ministries.

To request Jack Redmond as a speaker for your event or to learn more about available resources, please go to www.4thgen.org.

Become an Infusion Partner

Infusion Partners – Infusing the power, purpose and plans of Jesus into our culture!

If you wish to support Fourth Generation Ministries through prayer or financial support, please go to our website: www.4thgen.org. You may also send financial support or contact us directly by mail or phone at:

Fourth Generation Ministries
P.O. Box 376
Rockaway, NJ 07866
973-954-4227